THE OAKWOOD PRESS

CW00448543

The
Whipsnade and Umfolozi Railway
and
The Great Whipsnade Railway

by
C.S. Thomas

THE OAKWOOD PRESS

© Oakwood Press & C.S. Thomas 1995

British Library Cataloguing in Publication Data
A Record for this book is available from the British Library
ISBN 0 85361 478 4

Typeset by Oakwood Graphics.

Printed by Henry Ling Limited, The Dorset Press, Dorchester.

Front cover: Superior is shunting coaches at Whipsnade Central in this 1994 view, passengers only use the platform on the right of the picture, the other side of the loop being used for coach storage. *Author*

Rear cover, top: Excelsior takes water in Whipsnade Central station. *Peter Newman*

Rear cover, bottom: Autumn 1994 and Superior crosses Central Avenue at the end of the journey. *Carrie Thomas*

Published by
The Oakwood Press
P.O. Box 122, Headington, Oxford OX3 8LU

Contents

Chapter One

Introduction

Nature of the Railway

A narrow gauge steam locomotive with its train moves slowly along, excited passengers looking out from open sided coaches across rolling grasslands populated by axis deer and nilgai. To one side is a water hole where several barasingha are cooling off in the summer heat, to the other side a group of blackbuck glance up before moving on their way. This must be somewhere in Asia, India perhaps? Not at all, the meadows are in Bedfordshire and the train is headed by a locomotive built to serve the paper mills at Kemsley in Kent. This is the Great Whipsnade Railway at Whipsnade Wild Animal Park not far from Luton.

The railway has operated for nearly twenty-five years and yet seems to have been virtually ignored by writers and historians. It can hardly be said to have remained undiscovered all this time, passenger figures of 100,000 a year or thereabouts testify to the popularity of this two mile railway which offers something probably unique with its historic narrow gauge equipment and a journey shared for almost its full length with wild animals from across the world. Perhaps the fact that the railway operates as an additional attraction within the world famous Whipsnade Zoo, now Whipsnade Wild Animal Park, has led to the feeling that 'it is not a real railway'; if so, this is a great pity, for it is a real railway in every sense. The locomotives originate from historic industrial railways, one of which carried passengers, and represent types which can no longer be seen elsewhere. It is operated professionally and fulfils its purpose as a source of enjoyment to huge numbers of passengers. What difference is there from any other 'preserved' railway, each of which serves its public in its own way?

The railway was conceived by railway enthusiasts who had the necessary financial resources to build and equip it, and it has been a home for the rescue and renovation of locomotives and rolling stock belonging to others periodically throughout its life. There has never been a 'standard' narrow gauge in Britain, although many would argue the case for the nominal 2 ft gauge following the example set by the Festiniog Railway. But even Charles Spooner of that railway would probably have advised against using quite such a narrow gauge. The 3 ft gauge, which was adopted in the Isle of Man and to such a great extent in Ireland, did not find much support in England beyond the Southwold Railway. The 'middle' solution, however, of 2 ft 6 in. found favour with a number of railways. Now lost to us are the Leek & Manifold Valley Light Railway and the short-lived Sutton & Alford Tramway. The gauge was also the choice of the Pentewan Mineral Railway and the extensive complex of military lines at Broughton Moor. Also gone is the Chattenden & Upnor Admiralty Railway, although one of its locomotives has found its way to Whipsnade, which leaves us with the Sittingbourne & Kemsley Light Railway (direct successor to the Bowaters Industrial Railway), the Welshpool & Llanfair Railway and the Great Whipsnade Railway (formally Whipsnade & Umfolozi Railway) as representatives of the 2 ft 6 in. gauge. In the case of the Whipsnade Railway, it also has the highly appropriate distinction of sharing its location with a zoo which pioneered new ground in the keeping, breeding and conservation of endangered animals. Many of the hundreds of thousands who have travelled on this unique line will recall it by the early name of Whipsnade & Umfolozi, believing this is where the equipment came from. As we shall see, this is not correct, although to some degree it could have been, but the African connection is real enough in other respects. Under a new name the railway now shares its tracks with the animals of Asia and looks forward, one hopes, to the next twenty-five years of operation.

The Bowater's Paper Railway

Between 1904 and 1908, three steam locomotives arrived in Kent to work on a railway connecting the paper manufacturing mill at Sittingbourne with the wharves at Milton Creek. The third of the engines was named *Excelsior* and this was the start of what was to become a significant 2 ft 6 in. narrow gauge industrial railway system centred on the paper operations of Edward Lloyd Ltd. The official start of operations on this line is said to have been in 1906 but the wharves became inadequate and the company commenced construction of a new dock at Ridham on the Swale in 1913. The railway was extended to cover the three and a half miles between Sittingbourne and the new dock. In 1924, Lloyds opened a new paper mill at Kemsley, beside the railway and roughly mid-way between Sittingbourne and Ridham Dock. As a result, the use of the railway increased and more locomotives were purchased. The traffic consisted of wood pulp, china clay and manufactured paper. The railway also operated a passenger service for the Lloyd's employees which ran right round the clock and to a published timetable. Because of the loads of paper and the surroundings of the paper manufacturing plant, all the locomotives were equipped with spark arresting apparatus, the chimneys having the appearance of American 'balloon stacks'. In September 1948 the company was absorbed into the Bowater Group, becoming Bowater Lloyd Pulp and Paper Mills Ltd and in 1955 was changed again to Bowater's United Kingdom Pulp and Paper Mills Ltd. These changes made little difference to the railway; however, in 1965, a study of working practices reported that the railway should be replaced by road transport. The passenger trains were reduced in length and finally ceased to operate in September 1968. This was followed by the announcement that the railway would close completely in the Autumn of 1969. The railway had become well known to enthusiasts and was treated with affection by the staff, and we are fortunate that the management of the company felt that at least a part of the line should be preserved.

On the official closure of the railway for industrial purposes in October 1969, a section of the railway was leased to the Locomotive Club of Great Britain at a nominal rent, along with some of the locomotives and rolling stock, to form the

Sittingbourne & Kemsley Light Railway.   This preservation line operates between Sittingbourne and a terminus near the Kemsley mill known as Kemsley Down. Of the remaining locomotives, *Monarch* went to the Welshpool & Llanfair Railway (since sold again) and four others, together with a number of the bogie wagons, found their way to Bedfordshire where they were to form the nucleus of the new Whipsnade & Umfolozi Railway. Thus, arising from the closed industrial railway are two passenger railways where people can enjoy the sight and sound of preserved steam locomotives. The train rides on each railway are, however, dramatically different in their surroundings!

Chapter Two

Whipsnade Zoo

The Country Home of London Zoo

The Zoological Society of London (ZSL) was established in April 1826 and opened London Zoo in Regents Park, one of the oldest and most famous zoos in the world, to its members the following year. In 1847 the zoo was opened for the first time to the general public. Although the founders considered that the cause of science was the most important reason for the existence of the Society, the zoo was a huge success with the visiting public. The problem at Regents Park, however, is the limited size of the site, some five acres in the corner of a park in central London. Although substantial rebuilding has taken place over the years, eliminating old cages and poor animal houses, and enrichment programmes have been implemented to improve the lives of the animals, there is little doubt that the animals are 'on display' in enclosures which allow little scope for them to develop in natural surroundings.

In 1903, Sir Peter Chalmers Mitchell became the Secretary of the London Zoological Society, a post he was to hold until 1935. He was a visionary who had already broken new ground in the concept of displaying animals in surroundings other than cages, with the construction of the Mapin Terraces at Regents Park. Now he was to pursue a project which would celebrate the Society Centenary. Sir Peter saw that the numbers of animals in the wild was already dwindling and dreamed of a large country park where animals could live in open surroundings and not in cages. He saw such a park as an addition to the conventional city zoo and the creation of large natural wildlife reserves and, controversially for that time, he believed exotic animals would be more healthy in the open air than inside heated houses.

Many possible sites were looked at until a derelict farm of some 500 acres on Dunstable Downs was found. The estate was badly neglected and much work was needed, but the decision was made to purchase it in December 1926. The first animals arrived in 1928 and by 1931 what we now know as Whipsnade was ready for opening to the public on 23rd May. Something had been created which was different from anything else in Britain or the world - an open country zoo where wild animals from around the world could live in spacious open air surroundings.

Changing Face of Zoo Parks

The opening of Whipsnade coincided with a warm Whitsuntide and with newspaper headlines such as 'Biggest Zoo in the World', 'The Jungle of England' and '500 Acres of Freedom', people flocked to this new kind of zoo. On the Bank Holiday Monday after opening 27,000 people headed for the zoo and cars jammed the roads for miles around, the police even stopped London trains from going to Luton. Whipsnade was not only a new kind of zoo, but it coincided with a new level of mobility for the population. The railway network offered easy transport for all, coach outings were becoming popular and the age of personal transportation had arrived with increasing ownership of motor bikes. The mass production of cars, while not yet within reach of everybody, meant that the age of the car had certainly begun. In the early days cars were only allowed into the Park on Mondays, but at the beginning of the 1960s when the ownership of a car had become commonplace, they were allowed in every day of the week and in 1960, 30,000 cars were admitted to the Park.

It had always been envisaged that not only would animals roam freely around this new type of zoo, but that visitors should enjoy a clear view of the animals. The 1960s saw extensive work to achieve this objective with the construction of ditches combined with low barriers and the deliberate departure from 'traditional' wire and fences to contain the animals within their paddocks. In combination with, and partly as a result of, the ever increasing ownership of cars and new expectations for the conditions in which animals were kept and seen by the public, the period from the mid-1950s to mid-1960s saw a substantial increase in the number of zoos in Britain and, most significantly, the opening of the new 'Safari Parks' which took the concept a stage further. Not only did the animals have large areas in which to roam, but people were offered the opportunity to drive their own cars through the enclosures as well! Whipsnade may have been the first of its kind, but there was now stiff competition.

Conservation

In the first guide book for Whipsnade, Sir Peter Chalmers Mitchell wrote that the Park should be 'for the breeding of wild animals and a sanctuary for British wild birds and plants'. This objective remains and Whipsnade is one of the world's leading conservation centres, with successful breeding programmes contributing to the prevention of loss for ever of threatened animals and involvement in schemes to re-introduce animals back into the wild. The first recorded birth at Whipsnade was a muntjac deer in 1928 and has been followed by many other births which were the first of their kind in Britain including spur-winged goose (1933), Manchurian crane (1944), Indian rhinoceros (1957), snow leopard (1960) and cheetah (1967). The zoo was also home to ten species of animal in danger of extinction including Pere David's deer, Przewalski's wild horse, Indian rhinoceros and African black rhinoceros. It was with this background that Whipsnade were informed in March 1970 by the Chief Conservator in Natal that the park had been chosen as the first European breeding ground for the white rhinoceros.

At the turn of the century, the white rhinoceros was on the verge of extinction in South Africa, mainly as a result of poaching for their horns (actually compressed hair) which some people believed had aphrodisiac properties. By the 1920s only 20 or 30 remained, although now protected, in the Natal National Park. Following serious efforts to combat poaching, particularly in the

Zululand Game Reserve at Umfolozi, the numbers began to increase and the Natal Parks Board decided that to insure against possible future disasters, breeding herds should be established in other parts of the world. Whipsnade was chosen as the first white rhinoceros conservation centre outside Africa. Whipsnade had kept white rhinoceros before, but on nothing like the scale now envisaged. Fortunately, there was a large amount of undeveloped space available within the park which had never been open to the public. At the Studham end of the park was an area which had been brought into cultivation during World War II, much of it having become corn fields. This area was now prepared and landscaped to become the home of the white rhinoceros herd. The animals were transported in crates on the deck of the Union Castle ship *Kinnaird Castle* and all twenty (seven males and thirteen females) arrived at their new home on 5th August, 1970, where they were to join an existing pair which had been at the zoo since 1967, making a herd of twenty-two animals in all. As the rhinos stepped out of the crates and explored the new paddock, they may have noticed that home was shared by a single line of brand new railway track.

STOP PRESS

This new baby White Rhino has been named Mazinda. He is the first to be born in Great Britain, and only the second to be born outside South Africa.

Chapter Three

Construction Begins

Initial Proposals

The construction of a new railway generally requires a number of statutory approvals such as the making of a Light Railway Order or, in the case of older railways, Acts of Parliament. Whipsnade Park is, however, privately owned land and this allowed for a much easier birth for the idea of a new railway within the zoo.

The ideas for alternative transport systems within Whipsnade date back to the late 1950s, and early 1960s, when the Duke of Edinburgh had been keen on the idea of a monorail within the park. This idea was originally put to Mr Malcolm McAlpine, who was the uncle of Mr William McAlpine. This would have been a very advanced concept at the time, perhaps even ahead of its time, since in more recent years such transport systems have been built at a number of zoo collections. Then, however, the concept was costed and found to be far too high. The idea for a rail based transport system had however been planted and the next thought was for a 2 ft gauge railway, but this idea also faded away. In September 1968 outline proposals were prepared as part of a 'Draft report on Development of Whipsnade Zoo Park, Bedfordshire' for a 'Minirail'. It is not clear if this refers to the aforementioned 2 ft gauge railway idea, or was yet another proposal. In any event, the reasoning shown in the report is a useful indicator of the direction of thinking at the time. The proposal was for a system of about two miles in length, with a station at the main entrance and four others disposed around the park. Each of the outlying stations would form the nucleus of a 'centre' comprising animals houses, aviaries, catering etc. The minirail could be left or boarded at will, the ticket being of a 'rover' form. The most interesting section read, 'The Minirail would be extended with a loop about one mile long across the present farm area. Most of this area would be in effect one vast paddock with large herds, and would only be extensively visible by Minirail; on foot it would be visible from along one side.' In the event this scheme was not to come to fruition, but the section quoted is very close to describing what was to happen a few years later and provides further background to the eventual arrival of a narrow gauge railway in the park.

When the closure of the Bowater's Railway became known, Mr William McAlpine (later Sir William) purchased *Chevallier*, Mr Bernard Latham bought *Excelsior* and a quantity of other equipment of 2 ft 6 in. gauge became available. The Whipsnade authorities remained keen on the idea of a railway, particularly in the knowledge of the imminent arrival of the white rhinoceros herd, seeing such a line as the means by which the public might gain good views of the animals, since the new paddock was only accessible on one of the sides. With the availability of the Bowaters equipment which was not required for the Sittingbourne & Kemsley preservation project, along with *Chevallier*, all of which was sufficiently robust to stand a good chance of surviving a shared environment with animals as large as the rhinos, and the close connections with Regents Park and Whipsnade of Mr William McAlpine, all of the ingredients had begun to come together which would lead to building a new railway at Whipsnade.

Sir William McAlpine, widely known as 'Mr Bill', is the great grandson of Sir Robert McAlpine, a civil engineering contractor who pioneered the use of mass concrete as a building medium and achieved fame in railway circles for the work done by his company, Robert McAlpine & Sons, in building the Mallaig Extension of the West Highland Railway. Robert McAlpine appointed his son, Robert, to take charge of construction of the Mallaig line which commenced in 1897 with his younger son Malcolm as Assistant. In addition to continuing to run the famous construction business, Sir William McAlpine is a railway enthusiast and has an interest in zoology, being a Fellow of the Zoological Society of London and having served on the Society Council. At this point it is also appropriate to introduce the figure of Mr Tom Hill to the story. Mr Hill was, indeed still is, an employee of Sir Robert McAlpine Ltd and, at the time, was the personal assistant to Sir William. He was also a railway enthusiast, his main interest being in the civil engineering and operational side of railways rather than the historical aspects of the equipment. At a later date, Tom Hill was the owner of a commercial miniature railway along the seafront at Hastings.

Mr McAlpine wrote to the Zoological Society of London in April 1970 putting forward ideas for a suitable railway and the arrangements proceeded by way of a series of letters exchanged between Mr Tom Hill, on behalf of Mr McAlpine, and the Zoological Society. By the beginning of May the proposals were becoming more developed and on 4th May, 1970, Mr Hill wrote to the Society and submitted more detailed information on the proposals for financing and construction of the proposed 2 ft 6 in. gauge railway in Whipsnade Park. Underlying the proposal was the idea that the operation would be at no cost to the Society. Mr McAlpine and Major the Hon. Jeremy Monson would form a company and put up the necessary capital for the construction and running of the railway. To offset this, the company would collect and retain the fares and the zoo would receive an annual rent of £250. The initial estimate of capital expenditure was £41,400 and the predicted income for the summer period was £15,000, assuming a zoo attendance of 500,000 and the railway carrying a maximum of 7,500 passengers per day in the summer season.

This initial proposal was that the company would operate for a ten year period, at the end of which the future would be mutually agreed, the agreement would also be the subject of a review after two summer seasons. The two year review was naturally a source of concern since a part of the capital would represent non-recoverable costs and would also involve expenditure of some £5,000 in removal and re-instatement costs. It was therefore specifically requested that such a removal would only be 'in the unlikely event of it causing distress to the animals.' There were various headings which would require detailed decision and agreement, including the site of the railway, service to be provided, fares, buildings, reviews, insurance and advertising. The letter closed in the hope that sufficient information had been given 'for you to make an early decision in order that construction may commence.'

The Zoological Society replied on 8th May, 1970, and the main body of the letter is worth quoting in full.

> The proposals in the letter have been considered by the Society and they are accepted in principle, subject to there being a complete review of any agreement made between the railway company and the Society after two years. It will also, of course, be necessary to agree detailed terms under the heads which you listed in your letter and any others which may be relevant. In practice, however, this means that the Society agrees to the railway company going ahead with construction, provided Mr McAlpine and his partner are able to accept the two-year review.

This letter was quickly followed up by a meeting on 11th May, between Mr Hill (representing Mr McAlpine and Major Monson) and Miss Owen and Mr Rawlins for the Society. A number of agreements were reached which Mr Hill summarised in a letter dated 26th June, 1970. The review after two summer seasons had been agreed to, the operation in the interim being referred to as an experiment, but the Society had agreed that it would not insist on removal of the railway at the end of this period 'unless it has caused distress to the animals or detracted from the zoo operations or image, and even then, except in the extreme circumstance, the Zoological Society would permit the railway to run down over a further 2-3 years in order that the Company might recover its capital.' The company also reserved its right to suspend operations and remove the track if the operation was not commercially viable. The intention was that at the review a contract would be drawn up to continue operation of the railway for a further period, making ten years in total, after which the future would be decided by mutual agreement. The letter continued, 'Further, at the first review period, it will be considered by both parties whether the railway should be extended round the zoo to form an additional attraction and/or a transport system. This consideration also subject to gaining necessary planning permission.' The company proposed to commence running the railway 'as soon as possible this year and at Easter in 1971 and running until the end of September.' The intention was to run a service between 11.00 am and 6.00 pm each day, with the right to close for one day per week, and to run services at the discretion of the company in the remaining months of the year. The question of fares was to be at the discretion of the company and the annual rent would not be paid prior to the first review period. It had also been agreed that the railway company would set up a souvenir shop 'in the forecourt to the station adjacent to the children's zoo', thus showing that by now the site of the station, and probably the route, had been agreed. It is also interesting to note that Mr Hill raised an item which had not been mentioned previously by requesting 'that enthusiast and kindred group excursions to visit the zoo and travel on the railway enter the zoo for a special rate by mutual agreement', thus allowing for the theme of volunteer and enthusiast support which would subsequently become very much a part of the railway's early life. The letter closed with confirmation of the form of agreement which would apply for the initial stages, 'Everything is set out in this letter to comply with the agreement that prior to the first review the Company will operate under an exchange of letters in lieu of a formal contract.'

The response from the Society came on 22nd July, 1970, and was a quite long and detailed letter setting out the Society's position. The experimental railway arrangements were to be reviewed in the autumn of 1971 and the Society was anxious to ensure that the railway company should not acquire a lease, tenancy or interest in any part of the land at Whipsnade, therefore the use of the word 'rent' was deemed inappropriate and the term 'licence payments' was to be substituted. The erection of a souvenir kiosk (and any other buildings) and the operation of the whole scheme 'must, therefore, be dealt with under licence from us - as was the laying of the track.' The inference of this statement is that by now the rails had already been laid even though the full details had not been finalised. Clearly this indicates goodwill on both sides during the negotiations, as well as explaining how the railway was able to start operations by the August of that year. The letter continued with details about the allocation of expenses such as rates, water and electricity within the licence payments, and makes it clear that the question of termination of the experiment remained a matter for the Society and that in the event the circumstances were sufficiently serious to cause them great concern they could not agree to permit the railway to continue for the additional two to three year run down period. The request to close for one day a week was agreed to, but with the suggestion that this never be a Saturday, Sunday or Public Holiday (except Christmas Day) 'as it would not be in the interest of the Society or the Company to withdraw services on these busy days.'

In the meantime, the Ministry of Transport had been contacted and they replied on 30th July, 1970, to the effect that since the railway was to run entirely over private land with no interference with public roads or rights of way, no Light Railway Order was necessary. This letter, along with the letters of 22nd and 24th July, 1970 (the latter was a correction of a minor mistake in their previous letter) were considered by the solicitors acting for Mr Hill. They wrote to him on 17th August, confirming that they found nothing to object to in the Society's proposals and suggested that the arrangements now be summarised in a licence agreement to cover the first two years' operations, with a more comprehensive negotiated contract or agreement after that. On 29th September the solicitors wrote again to Mr Hill, enclosing a draft letter which drew all the threads together into a single document to summarise the correspondence which had taken place and to form the agreement between the two parties to be forwarded for final confirmation. The experimental period was to end on 30th September, 1971, at which point the arrangements would be reviewed and consideration given to the extension of the railway. By the time of this letter, however, the railway was already an operating concern.

Pleasurerail

Pleasurerail was a private company whose directors were all railway enthusiasts. The company was legally formed on 5th October, 1970, with the objective of constructing steam railways in suitable locations on which vintage or new stock would be operated, the initial line to be operated being the Whipsnade and Umfolozi line. The company was formed by Mr William McAlpine (later the Hon. Sir) and Major the Hon. Jeremy D.A.J. Monson who were the largest shareholders, and Mr Gerry Germing. The company secretary was Mr F.H. Flack of Messrs John M. Winter & Sons, the company auditors. The Directors also included Mr Thomas B. Hill, who became Managing Director of the company, and Mr Robin Butterell. The leading directors provided the initial funds to meet the costs of constructing the Whipsnade line which continued apace during the summer of 1970, prior to the formal formation of the company, but Pleasurerail was always intended to be a profit making company which had to earn its keep by the generation of revenue. As it turned out, the initial bank loan to set up the operation took considerably longer to pay off than first anticipated and accounts to some extent for the reluctance of the company to become involved in further extensions to the line in later years.

In addition to preserving historic locomotives, the policy of the company was to promote any viable form of rail transport and in the early 1970s was developing a monorail system which got as far as producing and testing a prototype with a view to going into production, the trial unit being installed at Beaulieu Motor Museum. It should be noted, however, that the monorail at this site now is not the same system, the eventual installation having been provided by a different company. A further proposal, prepared by Tom Hill was for a very sophisticated monorail system which would have served Regents Park Zoo and included a spur to connect with an underground station and bridging the road around the park to link the two London Zoo sites. This idea was not approved for several reasons and eventually all the monorail schemes died away. For a time, the company changed its name to Linehaul Systems Ltd while pursuing these other projects, the original name being thought to sound somewhat 'amateurish'. The change took place in early 1976, the new name being intended to provide a more serious sounding operation, although Pleasurerail was retained as a registered business name. The name of Linehaul was discontinued on 28th April, 1983, when the company reverted to its original title of Pleasurerail Ltd.

As well as operating the railway at Whipsnade the company also operated a railway in the grounds of Knebworth House in Hertfordshire at around the same time. This was to a nominal 2 ft gauge and was known as the Knebworth Park West Railway. It consisted of about one mile of track incorporating a shunting loop in the station area plus three sidings, then a straight section which in turn led to a large circular loop around part of the grounds, access to which was by a spring-loaded point. The railway was eventually purchased by Knebworth House itself, the Pleasurerail manager being transferred to the new owner's staff. This line was closed when the land was required for other purposes.

Later, a further railway was built and operated at Blenheim Palace. This was a 15 in. gauge miniature railway, as opposed to narrow gauge, and operated steam locomotives on an 'out and back' line. This railway was also sold to the site owners.

By 1990, the only remaining activity of the Pleasurerail company was at

Whipsnade. Pleasurerail ceased trading on 5th November, 1990, when the railway was taken over by the zoo. The Directors changed little over the years, at the time they formally resigned from office they consisted of Sir William McAlpine, Mrs J. McAlpine, Major Monson, Mr Germing and the Company Secretary, Mr Flack. As far as the Whipsnade Railway is concerned, this is to jump ahead of the story.

Experimental Line Built

The new railway was built during the summer of 1970 under the direction of Mr Tom Hill who acted as the line's Engineer. While the detailed negotiations referred to above were continuing, Mr Hill surveyed the site and drew up the plans for the route and fixtures and managed the project through to completion. The area for the new paddock was at that time simply a grass field, although part of the zoo, and the men working on the line were watched by small deer and wallabies which were free to roam all over the zoo park. Fortunately, a record of construction was made on 16 mm film and shows the progress of the building work. A small team of men, together with two caterpillar diggers, one with a trenching bucket at the back, levelled out the route for the new railway across virgin field. This was followed by the ballast which was delivered to the site by large trucks and spread out over the new formation. This first stretch of line only required a single ha-ha, a design of bridge combined with a fence and ditch devised by Tom Hill to allow the railway to enter the paddock whilst preventing the animals from escaping. The support at the yard end was formed by digging out the soil and then filling with ready mixed concrete delivered from a large cement lorry with the normal revolving mixer on the back. The ditch was dug out in front of the concrete support ready for the bridge. The steelwork for the bridge itself was delivered to the site already built and was dragged off the lorry by one of the diggers positioned on the far side of the ditch. The other digger was used as a form of crane, the steelwork being suspended from the digging bucket and the bridge manoeuvred into place. The caterpillar diggers were used throughout as makeshift cranes, rails, etcetera, being slung from ropes or wires off the digger buckets whenever heavy materials needed to be moved around the site. The railway sleepers were placed by hand, levelling and packing being done in the time honoured fashion with spades and a spirit level, together with a man jumping on a sleeper to 'pack' it into place when required! It is also interesting that holes were bored into the sleepers, certainly when laying the points, by hand. Obviously there was no power available and no portable source was used either.

By the end of June 1970, the curve into the station beside the children's zoo was complete, together with the point which was to lead off into the yard complex, although at this time there was only a short length of siding heading in the general direction of the site which was to become the shed. This was still grass and the workers were accompanied by horses, sheep and at one point a camel, who all enjoyed the grazing beside the new railway! There was a second point a little further along and the tracks thus separated into two parallel lengths down into the site of the station. There are two interesting details to note about this formation. Firstly, the continuation of the curve into the station in the form of the 'main line' led into the track to the north side of the station to be (the children's zoo side), the track on the south side was the siding with the turnout coming off the line of the curve distinctly to the left as one faces the station area. Having turned off the main line, this siding immediately curved right again to then parallel the other track into the station. The other detail is that when first laid, both tracks in the station were of conventional construction onto the earth base, and not laid on the continuous concrete base which can be seen now. The area of the park near the children's zoo and out round the curve towards the copse had always been known to retain water and become very 'boggy', in fact this section has always provided problems for the railway. After the first season's operating, the tracks in the station area started to subside, the ground under them being described as like a sponge full of water. About 12 to 18 months after the opening, these tracks were stripped out and the concrete slab was laid throughout the station area. The tracks were then relaid onto this base. To return to the situation in June 1970, the significant event was the arrival of *Chevallier*. The locomotive arrived on a low-loader, chimney facing the back of the vehicle. The loader was reversed down the slope to the end of the station track and the wheels removed from the truck. The next operation was physically to lift the track, with sleepers attached, and pack it in a slope up to the level of the locomotive with further sleepers and wood. Lengths of rail were then cut to length with a torch, holes for fishplates being also burnt through the rails, and thus a track was built up onto the low-loader to allow *Chevallier* to be rolled down onto the rails. When *Chevallier* was safely down on the firm track she was then towed clear behind a cable attached to the ubiquitous digger! The whole operation was viewed by fascinated visitors in the children's zoo who received an unusual bonus attraction to their day out! The arrival of the locomotive also received coverage in the local paper published on 8th July, 1970, the men who had done the job on a hot sunny day being photographed standing on the buffer beam, tanks and boiler of the locomotive.

The next operation was the collection and arrival of the two signal boxes. This was carried out on one day by the same gang of men with a crane and two low-loader trucks. Both boxes were of wood construction and still mounted on brick 'plinths' which formed the ground floors at their existing standard gauge railway sites on the Leighton Buzzard-Linslade line and both were located adjacent to level crossings. There remains some confusion as to precisely where the original sites of the boxes were. One came from the crossing at Wing, near Leighton Buzzard, but publicity for the railway tended to refer to buildings 'from Linslade'. Unfortunately, this was actually more to do with marketing than categoric fact, the idea being to capitalise on public interest in the location of the Great Train Robbery, implying some connection with the buildings now at Whipsnade. The first box to be collected was that which would become the Whipsnade Junction box on the curve by the yard. Before being lifted, the gang knocked out all the windows and then proceeded to pull away the rotted guttering. Cables were slung from girders placed under the floor of the box through holes knocked through the supporting brickwork and attached to the crane jib without any spreaders. The box was lifted off the brick base, with the cables pressed up the sides and against the eaves of the box, the whole building appearing to be in some danger of collapse as it rose into the air. If the gutters had not been removed previously, they certainly would have been with this treatment! Having got the box onto the lorry, which was placed across the level crossing during the operation, the group then moved to the other box situated a short distance away. This building was to become the station booking office and souvenir shop. The removal was not so drastic in that the glass was left in place this time. However, as the crane started to lift, it became clear that something was still attached underneath. This problem was resolved by one of the party clambering underneath the suspended building with a pick axe, protected only by a flat cap, and knocking away the obstruction! It is interesting to compare these operations with that to recover the Soham box some twenty years later. Everybody in the vicinity of the Soham operation was equipped with hard hats and high visibility vests and the box was moved by cables attached to the ends of girders passed underneath the floor of the building. A clear reminder of the influence of health and safety legislation for both personnel and the building! Some amusement was generated by one of the party who stood inside the box and waved a green flag as he 'steered' the wheel which would have operated the crossing gates and was still located inside the building as the lorry slowly pulled away for the journey to Whipsnade. In fact Tom Hill, who was in charge of the operation, admits it 'may well have been' he who was the person concerned! When the convoy arrived back at the park the first box to be placed was that for the station. This operation was quite straightforward, the transporter simply manoeuvring down to the site and the box lifted off and placed with the front facing south on a low pre-prepared plinth at the end of the two railway tracks. Attention then turned to the box for 'Whipsnade Junction'. This was somewhat more difficult because of the access to the site. The arrival was both crude and slightly spectacular as the lorry simply drove through the line of trees at a point roughly near the present road/rail crossing on the circuit, the truck with a signal box apparently bursting through the foliage on to the grass on the railway side. The grass was not banked up as it is now, but nonetheless the progress of the truck with a decidedly rickety signal box on board lurching over the rough ground appears quite alarming on the film footage which has survived. All was well in the end, however, and the box was craned off into place on its own plinth. Both boxes were subsequently restored and re-painted at their new locations.

The work had proceeded very quickly in the newly created paddock, and was completed before the arrival of the rhinos from Umfolozi. The name of the new railway was selected by making the obvious connection of the site of the line, and the origin of the animals with which it would share the route - so 'The Whipsnade & Umfolozi Railway' it was to be. An advertisement for a manager of the new railway had been placed and was answered by Mr Trevor Barber who was appointed and arrived just after the main line had been completed. Mr Hill retained overall responsibility for the railway as Managing Director. Mr Barber was on the site and managed the day to day operation and mechanical side of the railway, including arranging publicity and the purchasing of souvenirs. The locomotive *Chevallier* was already at the site, together with ten passenger carriages, and work was still being done to complete the new railway ready for opening. The actual opening was a fairly low key affair with no great ceremony. The first train ran on 26th August, 1970, and was handled by *Chevallier* which pushed four carriages carrying about 120 people, including reporters and cameramen, out into the rhino paddock. The total track length on opening was about 1,000 yards and the line terminated with a sand drag just short of the fence at the far end of the rhino paddock, roughly where the line of the fence from the Onager paddock meets the railway today. At the end of the line was a signpost which pointed 'To Umfolozi 5,753 miles'. The fare in the opening season was 3s. (15 pence) for adults (14 years and over) and 2s. (10 pence) for children under 14 years and 'old age pensioners' to use the terminology of the period. Special party rates were available, as were special rates for schools, educational establishments and youth organisations which met specified criteria. The fare for the 1972 season appears to have remained at the same level. It is interesting to compare these figures with the price of admission to the zoo itself, which in 1972 cost 45 pence for adults and 25 pence for children. The car park cost 15 pence, but if you wanted to take your car into the park it cost an extra £1 on Sundays and Bank Holidays, 75 pence on other days in summer, and 50 pence and 25 pence respectively in the winter. Full time operations continued until ceasing for the winter on 30th September, 1970, although a meeting with the zoo on 25th September resulted in agreement that during October the railway would open on Sundays and Mondays and any other days on which Mr Barber and Mr Manton (the zoo curator) felt it would be right to do so in view of weather conditions, visitor numbers and special occasions. It was also decided to run a train at least once a fortnight in order to keep it in trim and the rhinos used to its presence. The railway was to resume full operation at Easter 1971 and continue until 30th September, 1971. The first step, building a railway, had been achieved. Now came the task of getting the other equipment into full working order and developing the potential of the new line.

The railway station was located behind the children's zoo, now the bird garden, and passengers for the railway would arrive from the road which runs at right angles to the tracks and walk down to the small booking office and souvenir shop. This was the signal box which is now on the south platform of Whipsnade Central station. The front had an opening section in the middle with a display of souvenir gifts for sale and, on the same side of the box as the door, a window opened up for the sale of tickets. The person on duty in the building sat behind the window and was able to turn from the same position and serve customers at the front. The station was painted green and yellow, and apparently matched the colour scheme of the passenger carriages. Over the following three years the range of items for sale was developed to include ashtrays, glasses, pens and bookmarks - all advertising that they came from the Whipsnade and Umfolozi Railway. There were even drawing books available with pen and ink drawings by Trevor Barber on the front cover, one for each of the locomotives, and separate reproductions were sold as individual drawings of each locomotive. After purchasing their tickets the passengers entered an enclosure behind the booking office which was fenced off from the two railway tracks which were separated by a low concrete built platform, the tracks themselves terminating at a buffer stop built up from timber and iron in a recessed area. Passengers waited in the holding area until an incoming train had stopped and unloaded, after which they were allowed through a gate on the right hand side of the white painted platform fence (other side from children's zoo) and on to the platform to board their train. The platform itself was divided down the centre by a similar white painted fence, presumably to allow loading of one train while passengers were leaving another on the other platform. Small white notices with black letters/numbers about mid-way along the platforms defined platform 1 as being on the north (children's zoo) side and platform 2 on the south side.

The railway tracks left the station, passing the signal box which was named 'Whipsnade Junction' but not operated as a signal box, actually being used as a store and mess room and which remains on the site today. At this point the line also passes the double arm semaphore signal, which was always a dummy and intended simply to add to the railway 'atmosphere'. From the signal box the actual track route is the same as it is today. The tight right hand curve which exits the yard has always been the cause of problems for railway staff. Even in the early years the formation tended to sink and on one occasion staff worked overnight to rebuild the formation in order for operating to take place the following day. The railway continued on its present alignment, but in those days there were animals kept in the fields on each side of the railway. It was possible for passengers to see Soay sheep on the other side of the line from the station, then past European bison and camels before reaching the first ha-ha. In the early years of the railway this was known as the 'Umfolozi bridge', and since the ditch was water filled a signboard was placed by the railway saying 'Umfolozi River'. At the time of opening this was the only ha-ha and on crossing it the line entered the rhino paddock. In addition to the rhinos, this paddock also housed ostrich, antelope and gnu. The railway continued through the paddock as far as the fence at the far end, just short of what subsequently became the site of the second ha-ha and terminated in a sand stop.

There were no loops on this first railway at either end and trains were operated on an out and back shuttle principle. Initially it seems that trains were operated with only one person on the footplate. On 16th August, 1972, Mr Barber wrote to Mr Hill, largely in response to the British Safety Council survey report (further details follow later) and added his own comment 'In the future we should have two man crews because at the moment we have no "dead man" control on the locomotives and should a driver be taken ill or faint a serious accident could result.' In addition there was a guard in the brake carriage at the other end of the train. A simple electrical system was arranged to allow communication between locomotive crew and guard by a system of bells. One bell meant go, two bells to stop, and a continuous ringing indicated an emergency of some kind. It seems, however, that in these early days trains may not always have had a guard. The aforementioned safety survey included the recommendation by the investigator that 'There should be a strict ruling which forbids passenger train movements without the authority of a guard who should travel at all times with the train.' The response by Mr Barber to Mr Hill to this recommendation was 'This is to be discussed.' A loudspeaker system was also fitted in one set of carriages by Mr Barber so that passengers could receive a commentary, exactly as is done today, although the system fell out of use for some years before being reinstated in about 1984. When a train reached the far end of the line it simply stopped and then retraced its path back to the station. The trains travelled at about 8 or 9 mph and the total journey time was about 12 minutes. A concern to the manager in these days was the behaviour of children on the trains. It seems that not only did they often sit on the sides of carriages and lean out, but were apt to cross between one carriage and another while the train was in motion. Although an accident was feared, fortunately none seems to have actually occurred.

At the opening of the railway the track layout in the yard was far more simple than now. In 1970, there was not even a locomotive shed and the only place for maintenance to be done was over the pit located behind 'Whipsnade Junction' signal box. The pit is still there although not used as such. Engineering work was at least made possible by the presence of a mobile workshop. This was an ex-RAF vehicle and was basically a workshop/caravan mounted on four wheels. The railway was not well equipped with machining or welding facilities, lots of enthusiasm tending to make up for the lack of equipment. The large standard gauge crane was on the site from the beginning and extensive use was made of it for moving coal as well as other items. It was also used extensively in the heavy rebuilds of the locomotives. Originally the crane was located on a dedicated track in the yard but a short time later it was moved to the dual gauge track which runs down the side of the shed, the movement being achieved by lifting its own track from behind section by section as it progressed. The water tower was the same as it is now, and in the same location at the far end of the platform, and beside it was a conveyor which was used for coaling the engines. The conveyor has long since been dismantled, although little pieces of it live on - in the form of thick rubber pads cut from the belt material which are slipped between the train couplings to soften the contact between vehicles! Drawings for a locomotive shed were prepared late in 1971, the exact date on which it was erected is not known, but it had still not been built in August 1972. Construction seems to have been started in the winter of 1972 and continued into spring 1973. By February 1974 it was reported that another coat of stain was required for the walls together with paint for the roof. The track layout in the yard had by this time expanded somewhat from the original, but again, by August 1972 had still not reached its final layout.

Although the railway maintained an outward image of professional service to its passengers - indeed, it had been conceived and built as a commercial enterprise - underlying it was the fact that it was basically operated by enthusiasts. There were only two full-time paid staff, Mr Trevor Barber who was the manager dealing with all day to day affairs, publicity and purchasing of gifts, together with his engineering talents on the equipment, and Gill Roberts who acted as his secretary and staffed the ticket/sales counter in the booking office. At the time of the opening the local paper featured three men as being drivers for the new railway, Frank Cefford and Wally Sear, both from Dunstable and George Woodland of Woburn Sands. They were all retired men and steam enthusiasts who took turns between driving, firing and being guard for the trains and they would have been employed for the operating season only. The first full time driver was Mr Peter Stanbridge who was subsequently to become Chief Engineer for the railway. At other times if the railway was short of a driver one of the part-time drivers at Knebworth (also run by Pleasurerail) would be sent over, certainly Keith Tyler who drove on his days off from his regular employment (and later to become a driver at the Welshpool & Llanfair Railway) recalls being asked to go to Whipsnade on occasion. These arrangements continued after the circuit was completed. Most other people who worked on the railway had full time jobs but were paid a nominal amount for helping out or were volunteers working at the railway for the weekend. In February 1971 two 15 year-old school boys named Rod McLeod and Martin Johnson started helping out by selling tickets, working on the track and acting as guard, but their greatest interest was in working on maintaining and renovating the locomotives. Their association with the railway lasted 5 and 9 years respectively, periods which were of benefit in their subsequent careers. As Trevor Barber became more busy with running the railway a qualified steam engineer was employed part-time to help with repair work. In this respect, the early years of the railway were exactly the same in spirit as the many other railway preservation projects which were coming up all over the country. To place this in the context of the period, it is worth recalling that the Welshpool & Llanfair Railway (also of 2 ft 6 in. gauge) had only been re-opened by a preservation society on 6th April, 1963, over a part of its original length and by 1972, passenger services were still terminating at Sylfaen Halt, well short of Welshpool itself. This spirit was deliberately fostered by the manager and in these early years Whipsnade Zoo meeting rooms were often used for railway enthusiasts' meetings and lectures. The yard sidings were built up by volunteers who came from everywhere, simply for the enjoyment of creating a piece of railway. In order to give some balance to the commercial side of the operation, however, Tom Hill was insistent that the people working on the railway were paid some sort of wage in order to retain a measure of management control. In this respect also, achieving a balance between business necessity and paid staff, against the requirement for volunteer labour, is exactly the same as the present day situation on most preserved railways. It is also the case that in the early years all concerned were on a learning curve, few, if any, of the key figures having had any previous experience of running a railway.

The locomotives at Whipsnade in 1970 included all four of the steam engines plus the small Ruston mine locomotive and the Motor Rail diesel. For various reasons, however, not all were available for use. *Chevallier* had only recently been rebuilt and was always available, but *Conqueror* was not able to be used until 1971. *Superior* does not seem to have been capable of use during the first few years, the locomotive suffering from a lot of problems. *Excelsior* did not run at all in 1970 but was used in 1971, but the frames of the locomotive were in a terrible condition. The locomotive was extensively rebuilt over the winter of 1971/72, with further work in 1973. Full details of this work are given in

Chapter Eight. Of the diesels, the Motor Rail was used for works and track maintenance trains, one of the more unusual operations for a railway performed by this machine being to draw one of the skip wagons slowly through the rhino paddock, with the 'driver' walking alongside collecting litter which was thrown into the wagon. If a rhinoceros approached, the driver smartly hopped onto the locomotive and beat a hasty retreat! The Ruston could not be made to operate successfully and was sold in October 1972. All of the steam locomotives were painted green at the beginning, full details of livery are given for each locomotive in Chapter Eight.

Three of the locomotives, *Conqueror*, *Superior* and *Excelsior* were placed on the rails facing into the station, *Chevallier* faced the other way. Photographs always show trains operating with the locomotive at the station end of the train, thus trains were pushed out of the station and drawn back, arrivals by *Conqueror*, *Superior* and *Excelsior* appearing to be 'normal' chimney first arrivals, whereas *Chevallier* would bring its train back bunker first. This arrangement seems surprising since the line was downhill throughout its length after leaving the station and one would have thought that the locomotive would be placed at the downhill end of the trains, which at this time had no continuous brakes, the carriages being equipped only with their hand operated brakes. The reason for working in this way is thought to be that the staff found there was less risk of de-railing a carriage while it was rolling downhill than when it was being pushed up the gradient. An ex-employee of the railway, although not at that time, feels that trains were not always handled in this way. It must be borne in mind that there was no loop so any reversal of this operating procedure would have involved some shunting with two locomotives. There is also the evidence of the runaway carriage to suggest that the photographic evidence is correct.

'The Rhino Line'

An early publicity poster for the railway advertised itself as 'The Rhino Line' and offered a daily service between 28th March and 31st October. The operating times were between 11.00 am and 6.00 pm on Bank Holidays, 12.00 noon to 6.00 pm on Sundays and 1.00 pm to 6.00 pm on weekdays. All four steam locomotives were advertised and souvenir tickets for all passengers were proclaimed. This poster must have been produced for the 1971 season, presumably the months quoted were a little advertising 'puff'. Hand written notes on the original, in the nature of amendments for the printer for the next year's version, imply that the following year's season would run from 26th March to 29th October and weekday trains would run until 5.30 pm rather than 6.00 pm. A Pleasure Rail Ltd (note the word Pleasurerail was printed as two words) 'flyer' for '1972 Presentations' did indeed offer train services between 26th March, and 29th October, 1972 with services on weekdays between 12.00 noon and 5.30 pm between 3rd July and 1st October and between 1.00 pm and 5.30 pm on remaining weekdays. Sunday operating throughout the season was between 12.00 noon and 6.00 pm and Bank Holidays between 11.00 am and 6.00 pm. The railway was termed the 'Whipsnade & Umfolozi Railway' and advertised trips to take 'you into the heart of WHITE RHINO LAND at Whipsnade Zoo' (capitals per leaflet). A footnote stated that weekend operations and special trips through the winter were planned using either diesel or steam power dependent on weather. The leaflet also gave operating details for the Knebworth West Park & Winter Green Railway, the other Pleasurerail operation. Other early publicity leaflets and stickers of various shapes and sizes invited people to 'Take the Rhino Run'. Certainly the railway was marketed much more energetically than has been the case in later years.

The first year's operations were considered to be a success and although definitive figures have not been traced, it is said that 23,000 passengers were carried in that first season. In the spring of 1971, a party was held as a slightly belated 'official opening' for staff, friends and the Directors of Pleasurerail and their guests. White rhino number 19 (they had not been given names at that time because there were so many of them!) had been pregnant on arrival at the zoo and by coincidence the party was held on the same day as the birth of Whipsnade's first baby rhinoceros which was named Mazinda - a happy event all round for the different occupants of the year old paddock!

Now the railway was an operating concern the biggest priority was to sort out the locomotive situation. The position with steam locomotives over the first three years has already been covered, but the need for a powerful diesel had been realised from the start. Indeed, at the meeting which had taken place with the zoo on 25th September, 1970, Mr McAlpine had suggested that if a suitable diesel could be obtained a single carriage train could be operated on an *ad hoc* basis throughout the winter. A large machine was certainly needed to extend the number of running days out of season when it was not worth steaming a locomotive and as a back up to the steam fleet. Mr Barber knew about the large 100 hp Fowler diesels, having seen them operating some years before at the cement works in Penarth, South Wales. The works railway had closed down in 1968 and the two remaining locomotives had been sold in 1969. One had gone to the Welshpool & Llanfair Railway and was in use there, the other had been purchased by the Welsh Highland Light Railway (1964) Company and was in storage. A letter in the railway files dated 27th October, 1970, from Messrs Andrew Barclay, Sons & Co Ltd noted that Whipsnade were hoping to purchase Fowler 4160004 in 'the near future' and confirmed that they held 'a reasonable stock of spare parts'. It went on to enclose notes on the 'Maintenance of Diesel Locomotives.' The approach to buy the Welsh Highland engine was, however, turned down although some negotiations were still taking place in 1971, but it is interesting to note that eventually this locomotive did arrive at Whipsnade in 1975 to become *Hector*, but by then Mr Barber had left the railway. The search also included Africa, Mr Barber being in contact with the Sierra Leone Railway who replied in December 1970 that they were willing to help and asking what equipment was required. Although nothing came of this, it is interesting to recall that in 1975 a steam locomotive and four coaches were imported from Sierra Leone for the Welshpool & Llanfair Railway and eventually the locomotive came to Whipsnade, albeit for a brief visit, in 1993!

The search for a suitable diesel continued with various people in contact with Mr McAlpine concerning possible locomotives in Africa. The correspondence took an interesting turn in September when a Mr Frank Jux wrote offering various locomotives. The reply from Mr McAlpine on 15th September, 1970, said that he had a particular interest in finding a 2 ft 6 in. gauge diesel, asking if Mr Jux knew of any since 'I need it for the railway we are running at Whipsnade'. On the 17th Mr Jux replied that he was 'interested to hear recently of the Whipsnade & Umfolozi Railway' and went on to say that the Umfolozi Co-Operative Sugar Millers used to operate a number of 2 ft 6 in. gauge steam locos and still had a number of diesels. It seems from the tone of Mr McAlpine's reply that he had been unaware of this railway and said he would follow it up although the cost of transport may be prohibitive. He confirmed again 'I am looking for a large diesel and it would certainly be very appropriate to have one from Umfolozi', then explaining to Mr Jux how the name had been chosen for the Whipsnade Railway. Nothing further seems to come of these contacts, but on 6th September, 1971, the Hunslet Engine Co. Ltd wrote to Mr McAlpine to inform him that they had written to associates in South Africa asking if any diesel locomotives for 2 ft 6 in. gauge were known to be for sale. They particularly had in mind two types of their own manufacture which had been supplied to the Umfolozi Consolidated Sugar Planters Ltd, details of which were enclosed. Both were 0-6-0 machines, the larger being rated at 152 hp with dimensions of wheelbase 7 ft, length 17 ft 11 in. and weight in working order of 19 tons 6 cwt. The smaller locomotives were rated at 93-102 hp with dimensions of wheelbase 5 ft 2½ in., length 13 ft 9½ in. and weight in working order of 10 tons 15 cwt. The 'code word' on the order sheet was 'UMFOL'. Moreover, Hunslets continued 'one of the smaller locomotives was in fact named "Umfolozi".' The gauge of the Whipsnade & Umfolozi was selected because of the Bowater's locomotives and rolling stock and the name because the rhinos with which the railway was to share the paddock came from the Umfolozi area. What an astonishing coincidence that in the same area of Africa should be another Umfolozi railway, and of the same gauge!

It is unfortunate that the story does not end with a locomotive called 'Umfolozi' arriving from Africa but, in fact, the search for a diesel ended almost where it started, with an ex-Penarth Fowler. The full story of the acquisition of what was to become *Victor* is given in Chapter Eight, suffice to say here that the negotiations went very smoothly throughout, the only minor problem being that there was a very late change of plan concerning the delivery time at Whipsnade. Mr Smart of the Welshpool & Llanfair sent off a telegram more in hope than anticipation, but fortunately it was received by Mr Barber at 9.30 pm on the Saturday evening and he was able to get to the zoo on the following morning to receive the locomotive on Sunday 19th March, 1972. The new owners were clearly delighted with their acquisition and it is worth quoting a section in full from Mr Barber's letter to Mr Smart of 4th April, 1972.

The loco was off-loaded by about 11.30 am with no undue problems. The loco fits our requirements perfectly and looks part of the family already. We have carried out several trials on the locomotive and the major snag we came against was the poor braking. On examination we found that the blocks had been so little used that they were not bedded in. We have now corrected this and it is alright. Passenger carrying trials are well under way, last week a lad stalled it in the rhino paddock and the driver had not been shown how to start it.

The initial pleasure was not short lived either. On 19th June, 1972, Mr Barber wrote to Mr Smart saying *Victor* is a great locomotive and I wonder what we would have done without it over the last few months'.

It has been mentioned already that in these early days the railway had something of a preservation feel and approach. A number of the people who came along to help out were also interested in the Welshpool & Llanfair Railway and the proposal emerged to restore that railway's van No. 4. The offer was made to bring this vehicle to Whipsnade in January 1972, but there had been various problems and delays, including the person who was going to do the work having to be admitted to hospital. Nonetheless, in November, Mr Barber remained hopeful of finding someone else to take over the project. In the event, however, the idea did not work out, although it certainly gives an early indication of the quite close relationship which these two railways of the same gauge have enjoyed over the years.

In those early years there were, of course, the kind of mishaps which were alarming at the time but a source of amusement when recalled with hindsight. One of the coaches had been fully glazed and was used particularly in early spring, late summer and when the weather was bad. On one occasion, somehow it got loose onto the main line and started rolling off down the hill towards the rhino paddock, fortunately without any passengers on board. The staff gave chase on foot but had no hope of catching it as it gathered speed and careered right through the rhino paddock at about 30 mph, only coming to a stop when it hit the fencing at the far end of the line, where it punctured the heavy wire hawser fence which had been built to contain the rhinos. An alarming event centring on *Chevallier* occurred as a result of a slightly leaking regulator. A fitter dismantled the regulator to fix the problem and then re-assembled it. The following day, a Sunday morning, with the locomotive standing by the signal box steam was raised and the regulator gently opened. When nothing happened it was opened further, still nothing, nor did *Chevallier* show any sign of moving with the regulator wide open. By now the steam was blowing off and a rather horrible feeling came over Trevor Barber who closed the regulator and told everyone to get out of the way. Realisation then came that the locomotive was stuck at top dead centre so Mr Barber's brother applied a crow bar to the wheels to jerk the engine forward. Events then suddenly became a blur. *Chevallier* had taken off like a rocket and in seconds was doing about 30 mph off down the hill towards the rhino paddock! On recovering from this rather surprising turn of events, instinct took over and the regulator was moved from shut to wide open, and the reverser lever used to bring *Chevallier* to a stop. Further examination confirmed what had happened - the fitter had re-assembled the regulator crank the wrong way round, so 'closed' was actually 'open' and vice versa, the problem being compounded by the engine happening also to have stopped at top dead centre! As if all the above were not enough, when the story of the same incident was related to the author by another member of staff who was present an additional element to the events was recalled. This version has it that at some point, the runaway *Chevallier* actually hit a rake of coaches which was further up the line, and with the same effect as applies to the 'executive toy' which consists of several metal balls hanging from strings, where one ball hits the line, another bounces off the other end; apparently as *Chevallier* hit the coaches, the coach at the far end of the rake flew off on its own, separated from the rest with its coupling shattered! Could this in fact be the runaway coach already mentioned, for it would explain how the coach came to be loose and heading for the paddocks?

Generally speaking the rhinos did not worry about the train, but there was an occasion when a rhinoceros decided to ram *Excelsior*, and a rather more worrying incident when one went for a carriage and the train crew feared for a moment that the animal would hook its horn under the body and turn it over - the danger passed fortunately. On another occasion the train crew noticed that on one of the carriages the chipboard fascia panel which covered the ends of the transparent roof panels had come loose and started to slip down the upright roof supports. There was nothing to be done while in the paddock but watch with a combination of embarrassment and amusement as the panel slowly worked its way down to the passengers' eye level with people trying to look over or under the panel as the train continued on its way. Whilst the rhinos seemed happy enough with the train, a slightly surprising difficulty turned out to be the locomotive whistles. The local papers in July 1972 reported that residents of Whipsnade village were often asked 'where is the station' and the matter was taken up by parish councillors. It seems that *Victor* was the worst offender with one parish councillor being quoted as saying, 'The noise from this infernal diesel is deafening.' By February 1973 the paper was able to report that a meeting had taken place with the zoo when it was agreed that a less noisy whistle would be fitted to the offending engine and 'they had also said they would put it on the side of the engine farthest from the village.'

The survey of the railway was carried out by Mr S.A. Pearson of the British Safety Council on 27th July, 1972, and covered not only the Whipsnade line but the other railway operated by Pleasurerail at Knebworth. It opened with the encouraging comment about the Whipsnade & Umfolozi Railway that 'It has a professional appearance about it which may be improved by adopting the recommendations contained in this report.' This being in contrast to the section on the Knebworth West Park Railway which the inspector said '....does not appear to have been developed to the same extent. It does not have the same professional air about it as does Whipsnade.' The report continues by listing the motive power which consisted of the four steam locomotives, *Victor* and the Motor Rail (the Ruston having been sold by now) and confirms that all steam engines were stored in the open 'there being no covered area available for storage or maintenance'. The shed clearly had not yet been built but, in addition to the wheeled workshop, a 'general purpose machine shop' was now present on the site. By this time there were five sidings in the yard, each operated by hand levers. There followed a description of the rolling stock consisting of the ten coaches, each weighing 2½ tons and with fixed seating for 30 people. Then, as now, there were two set trains of five coaches. The couplings were described as of 'a combined double hook and buffer type, and there is a 1 in. diameter 5-link single safety chain fitted to one side of each coach.' Also, as has remained to the present day, the end coach of each train had a platform for the guard with a manual wheel braking system for that coach only, except that today with vacuum braking there is no need for a guard and the compartment is used instead for the volunteer giving the commentary. Also in the early days there was no actual seat fitted for the guard. The rolling stock summary is rounded off by noting there were a number of flat wagons, both with and without sides (these must have been ex-Bowater's wagons not yet converted) together with two side tipping wagons. The report continued with a description of the track and the station buildings and equipment.

The report then makes a number of detailed recommendations such as six monthly inspections of all couplings, the fitting of safety chains between locomotives and stock, together with double safety chains to the coaches and various other minor items. In relation to the permanent way there were a number of observations and recommendations, some of which would become familiar reading in later inspections! There was already evidence of 'sleeper slide' on the concreted areas and creeping and undulations on the main line. Reference was made to the 'unusual acute radius' of 'Bison curve' (this would be the sharp curve out of the yard past the double arm signal) and noted that check rails should be added with additional stays between the lines and larger spikes to be used on the inside rail. The lack of drainage for many sections of the line was also remarked upon. The inspector recommended the erection of signposts on the zoo service road (known as the farm crossing) to warn of passing trains. As it turned out, he was right, but the potential accident he foresaw did not happen until eighteen years later! Further detailed recommendations included securely clamping all facing points while trains were operating, improving the buffer stop facilities for the sidings and replacing the buffer stops in the station with a 'more substantial structure', also the provision of toilet facilities, which were non-existent. The inspector had obviously been informed of the plans which by now were being developed for the extension of the railway and he felt that they should include the introduction of automatic electric light signalling and vacuum braking for passenger trains. Mr Barber wrote to the inspector on 17th August, 1972, seeking clarification on some aspects of the report, but had already written to Mr Hill the day before giving a reply to each of the inspector's recommendations. Overall, the report seems to have been accepted as a fair assessment of the railway at that time with many responses being 'Accepted', in other instances the work had already been put in hand. It is interesting to note that in reply to the reference to automatic electric light signalling and vacuum braking for passenger trains on the extended circuit the response was 'This is already in hand.' The question of signalling has arisen on many occasions since but never implemented, and vacuum braking was not tested and passed as satisfactory until early 1987, and even then the installation was not complete until 1992!

The waiting arrangements at the station were the cause of some concern to a passenger who wrote in July 1972. He was worried that an arriving train could overrun the buffers and crash into the people waiting for their train, who would be unable to escape, enclosed as they were by the fencing. The letter was sent to Luton Rural District Council and resulted in an officer from the Council's Engineer and Surveyors Department visiting the railway to discuss the situation with Mr Barber. It transpired that the railway manager had already arranged for an inspector from the British Safety Council to inspect the whole railway to advise on any matters requiring attention and the report described above had not yet been received. In the meantime, work had already started on putting in a sand drag backed by railway sleepers at the point where the buffers were fixed. In fact, when Mr Barber wrote on 10th August, 1972, to the person who brought the subject up he was able to report that the sand drag would be completed on the following day, adding that such a drag had been debated for some time '... but as we are to extend the line this winter into a large circle we deferred the decision.'

Chapter Four

Expansion of the Line

Initial Success

The initial 1,000 yards of railway was built as an experiment to see if such a line could be a success and evaluate the potential for further expansion. By the summer of 1972, it was obvious that the railway was popular with the public and had been accepted by the animals. Work then went ahead to draw up plans for an extension of about a mile to link the railway into a continuous circuit. Luton Rural District Council wrote to the visitor who had expressed concern about the buffer stop arrangement at the station on 9th August, 1972, and closed their letter with the words '(I) have today received further plans to extend the railway further into the zoo and thus make a complete circuit with the line. No constructional details are shown but I am requesting information to prevent any further possible accident occurring'.

Line Extended and New Station Built

As with the initial line, Tom Hill did the survey for the extended line and designed the new engineering features. The plans had to fit in with fixed points defined by the zoo and so he did not have complete freedom in the design work, having to achieve the best result possible in the circumstances. The curves were laid to the maximum possible radius, but were still somewhat tighter than ideal and gradients were dictated by the topography of the available site. Work proceeded on the extension, paid for by Pleasurerail, and although not a McAlpine contract, the work was once again done with the help and advice of McAlpine resources. The construction was largely carried out using vehicles such as dumper trucks, etcetera, to move materials around the site, the railway's own stock apparently not being much involved, if at all. The work included building further ha-has to take the line through the additional paddocks and the new section of railway passed through areas which at that time housed zebra and eland in the enclosure which now houses the onager, and into paddocks occupied by deer and mouflon. The Round Close paddock at that time was the home of llama, nilgai and cranes. A level crossing was built to take the railway over Central Avenue and a tunnel was designed by Tom Hill to pass the line under Cut Throat Avenue. The tunnel was build by the 'cut and cover' method, the walls being pre-cast sections which were dropped into place following which the slab roof was placed on top to carry the road. When built, there was no ha-ha to prevent animals moving between Cut Throat and Round Close paddocks. The road layout at the junction of Central and Cut Throat Avenues was altered at this time, with a new grass area being laid out and the route for visitors' cars was now around the Woodfield paddock. Immediately to the east of the level crossing a new station was constructed which became Whipsnade

Central station. Two platforms were built, one on each side of the loop, which was formed on a curve. The signal box which had served as a booking office at the original station was lifted by crane onto an ex-Bowater's flat wagon and moved to the new site by *Chevallier*. It was placed to the south of the tracks by the crossing but was no longer required to serve its previous purpose. What is now the zoo shop building on the other side of the tracks was built to serve as a railway booking office, shop and waiting room and was completed by the end of 1973. The shop was also notable for the huge model of a rhinoceros which stood inside it. This was a fibre glass replica purchased at an auction by Sir William McAlpine in 1976 and arrived later that year, or early in 1977. The building was used in this capacity until 1990/91 when the inside was converted into purely a zoo shop and the booking office window was put into the back wall. It seems however that Pleasurerail ceased to run the shop in 1977. The zoo wrote to Tom Hill on 1st March, 1977, 'to confirm the quantities of stock removed from the railway shop a month ago.' An internal zoo memo, dated 10th June, 1977, refers to the zoo having taken over 'Mr Hill's stock and are selling these items now in our zoo shops.' It will be recalled that from the beginning the railway had sold a range of railway related souvenirs. It is not known exactly when this ceased, but it had certainly done so by early 1984.

Where the new railway continued up the slope, a footbridge for pedestrians was built, the line then crossed the road and joined up with the original tracks by Whipsnade Junction signal box. The old station was no longer to be used but the tracks, on the north side, remained to function as storage sidings. The main line arrived further to the south of the station tracks and a junction was made with the original line at the point where the turnout was located for the south side station line. To put it another way, a train arriving from the rhino paddock and taking the left road which previously would have led into the south platform, would now be on the new formation and heading for the road crossing. It has not been established for certain whether the original south line into the old station was definitely disconnected at this time; if it was not, an additional turnout would have to have been installed to connect into the newly constructed main line. On balance it seems unlikely this would have been done, far more likely that having been severed the south platform line was simply left disconnected, or even lifted in order to utilise the rails elsewhere on the new circuit. The new main line thus joined the main curve on an obviously tighter radius than that of the original curve. The new section of line adjacent to the old station was also laid on a concrete base in order to keep the new formation stable, following the lessons learned from the original experience of water logging in the station area. The whole scene at this end of the park was one of construction activity since the new dolphinarium (now the home of the sea lions) was opened in the same year just up Central Avenue adjacent to the new railway station. On the other side of the station was 'Wolf Wood', later this area was redeveloped into the present 'Tiger Falls' enclosure which was opened in 1991.

The railway was due to receive its first Royal visit at the beginning of August 1973 and most of the work, including the complete track circuit, was finished about six to eight weeks before the big day. The summer of that year was, nonetheless, one of urgent activity to get everything ready, 'a quite chaotic time' as one railway employee described it, with sweeping, cleaning and tidying continuing right up to the last minute. Her Royal Highness, the Princess Margaret, Countess of Snowdon attended the official inauguration on 2nd August, 1973, which was, of course, attended by the Directors of Pleasurerail. Whipsnade Central station was decorated with bunting and the Royal Train was hauled by *Conqueror* which looked resplendent decorated with a large red shield emblazoned with a crown mounted on the front of the smokebox. The shield was surrounded with flags of St George and the Union and there were three white lamps on the top of the buffer beam. The Royal train was preceded by *Excelsior* which acted as 'road checking engine', running light engine as in earlier times on the main lines, and the circuit was covered by *Excelsior* and the Royal train itself in an anti-clockwise direction. The Royal train had a guard, which was not always the case for public trains at this time, although there were normally two people on the locomotives. The guard for the special train was a 16 year-old schoolboy named Graeme Carr who had started with the railway in July 1973, working at weekends and during holidays. The payment when he started was £3 per day, by 1975 he was driving on the railway and the pay increased to £6 per day.

The locomotives remained placed on the rails as they had been from the beginning; with the circuit complete, this meant that *Conqueror, Superior* and *Excelsior* were now facing anti-clockwise while *Chevallier* faced clockwise. It is believed that *Victor* also faced anti-clockwise. The period just after completion of the circuit was a period of experimentation to explore the best methods of operating the railway. Some trains were run anti-clockwise, although the rather obvious problem was that of safely bringing a train to a stop in the station platform after the downhill approach from the yard and road crossing. The staff took no chances and always opened the level crossing gates on Central Avenue since the stopping point is only a few feet short of the road at this point. Trains were also run clockwise, which required all but *Chevallier* to run bunker first and on some occasions trains ran round the circuit consecutively in opposite directions, as one train arrived in the station from one direction, another set off in the other direction. All train control was done visually with no signalling and at least once there were actually three trains on the circuit at the same time. Running two, sometimes three, trains on the circuit is done now, but with the aid of radio communications and block sections under the supervision of a controller! By the end of the summer, and after the visit by Princess Margaret, the method of operating had settled down to a system basically the same as has continued to the present day. The use of clockwise running resolved the problem of stopping the train in the station on the downward slope. However, there was still the potential danger of a vehicle becoming detached from a train and rolling back down at speed into the station and the gates. In fact, if the gates were open and a runaway kept going through Round Close it would probably not come to a stop until well inside the rhino paddock - from the opposite direction! As we shall see, just such an incident was to occur the following year.

As well as the range of souvenir gifts which has been mentioned earlier, the

Although the negative is dated 1972, the author believes this picture of *Chevallier* was taken in 1970, and prior to the opening of the railway. Note the absence of fences on the platform, work taking place on the signal box and generally 'unfinished' air of the scene.   *Mervyn Turvey*

Superior meets a rhinoceros in a picture taken on 25th August, 1975.   *Mervyn Turvey*

On the morning of 2nd August, 1973 *Conqueror* on the left is ready to haul the Royal train while *Excelsior* waits alongside to act as 'road checking engine'
Author's Collection

Superior faces a Llama in Round Close on 25th August, 1975.
Mervyn Turvey

Sharp, Stewart & Co. class '7' 4-8-0 locomotive owned by David Shepherd displayed in the south platform of the original station which was no longer needed when the circuit was opened.

Nick Robey

Behind the locomotive was the Rhodesia Railways sleeping car No. 1808, which formed the other major element in the Zambezi Sawmills display. The north platform of the old station was still available for storage of Whipsnade stock.

Nick Robey

Excelsior, in green livery, the picture thus believed to date from 1971, returns with a train and rounds the curve before passing the yard and entering the old terminus.   *Trevor Barber*

Although of poor quality, this picture from 1973 is included since it is the only one so far found showing the Motor Rail locomotive. Note also that the dividing fence down the platform of the original station is still present, later it was removed and the platform became a staff car park until the arrival of the Zambezi stock in 1975.   *Graeme Carr*

Excelsior brings her train through Round Close paddock on 27th July, 1977. At that time the paddock housed llama and crowned crane as well as deer.　　　*Zoological Society of London*

Excelsior in Round Close paddock approaches the end of the circuit on 27th July, 1977.
　　　　　　　　　　　　　　　　　　　　　　　　Zoological Society of London

On Sunday 28th October, 1990, *Superior* decorated with a laurel wreath and black headlamp, approaches the farm crossing with the last train under Pleasurerail ownership. *Frazer Crawley*

Chevallier pictured on the Welshpool & Llanfair Railway during her 1991 visit, the first wagon in the train is loaded with the Whipsnade Land Rover! *Frazer Crawley*

On arrival from Welshpool *Dougal* is unloaded at the old station for the 1992 'Steam Up' weekend.   *Frazer Crawley*

An unusual view showing *Excelsior* working a 'Goods' train of Broughton Moor stock on 2nd May, 1993 during that year's 'Steam Up' weekend. The train has left Central station and is passing the Bear Trail, a number of the 'Steam Up' exhibitors are in what is normally the car park.   *Alti-Cam, Kent*

Conqueror leaving the Rhino paddock *c.* 1981/83.   *Author*

Chevallier waits at Central station for departure in Summer 1994, note the crossing for staff use between platforms and the stand pipe with short hose for watering the engines.   *Author*

shop also sold railway books and magazines and by 1973, a small visitors guide book had been produced. This was a 12 page booklet published by Pleasurerail Ltd entitled *The Whipsnade & Umfolozi Railway* and was prepared by the railway manager, Trevor Barber, and R.D. Butterell. The covers were in colour, on the front a picture of *Excelsior* and on the back a coat of arms. The contents included a map of the railway and a number of black and white photographs of the railway. There was a short introduction to the railway and it should be noted that an error crept into the production in that the date of the first train is given as 1971, not 1970. Readers may be assured that the author has discussed this with Mr Barber and careful comparison of personal and railway records has resulted in agreement that 1970 is the correct year! The booklet continued with a brief description of the route of the full circuit and it is interesting to note that this is described as travelling in an anti-clockwise direction - clearly produced during the early summer period of experimentation. There followed a page for each locomotive giving outline technical details and a large picture of each. Also available in the 1970s were colour postcards of the railway. The series included cards showing *Excelsior* and *Conqueror* in the station on the day of Princess Margaret's visit, *Excelsior* on the level crossing, *Victor* in orange and black livery, *Conqueror* taking a train through Round Close and *Chevallier* crossing a ha-ha with two rhinos in the background. There was also a card, measuring some 14¼ in. by 4¾ in., with a black and white picture of *Chevallier* and four carriages with a large part of the rhinoceros herd in the foreground, which was almost certainly taken in the very early days on the original out and back line.

By the end of the 1973 season the railway had achieved its present length and all four steam locomotives were useable. *Chevallier* and *Conqueror* were now running very well, *Conqueror* particularly being remembered as 'a beautiful, docile engine'. Following her extensive rebuilding *Excelsior* was also now running well in its new brown livery. A special effort had been made to get *Superior* into action for 1973 and in the summer of that year she was even fitted with a straight chimney. The condition of the locomotive was not good, however, and the engine was not used in regular traffic. In the autumn of 1973 *Superior* was stripped down and following extensive work was available for revenue earning service by the summer of 1974.

It will be recalled that with goodwill on all sides, the initial line had been built before the actual operating agreements had been finalised, the paper work being sorted out after the railway opened. The same situation applied again with the opening of the full circuit. The operating agreement between ZSL and Pleasurerail was actually dated 15th November, 1973, although it was deemed to have come into effect on 1st January, 1973, and to continue in force for a term of twenty years from that date. This document is crucial since it determined the conditions under which the railway operated until the eventual takeover by the zoo. Most of the terms and conditions were fairly straightforward, access of Pleasurerail staff and contractors to the zoo, free entry to the zoo for delivery of materials, use of zoo catering and toilet facilities, Pleasurerail to maintain the equipment in good condition, provide suitable indemnities, insurance etc. A clause was included to the effect that two years before the expiry of the agreement, both parties would consult as to future arrangements, and if they agreed on a continuance of the railway, a new agreement was to be negotiated. If no new agreement was reached, Pleasurerail were required to remove the railway and make good the site, including filling in cuttings etc. at their own expense. Pleasurerail were allowed to sell suitable railway souvenirs from a shop at, or near, the station with a percentage commission payable to the zoo. The route of the extension was defined, minor changes being allowed by mutual agreement, and the intention that the line should pass through areas containing wild animals was included. The railway was to be operated at no cost to the zoo, with a reasonable service during the summer season (Easter to the end of September) normally between the hours of 11.00 am and 6.00 pm, with the right to a rest day, but not on a Saturday, Sunday or Public Holiday. The winter service was to be commensurate with the number of visitors in the park making operation economic, but normally with a service at weekends provided the weather was reasonable. The right to charge, and revise, fares was with Pleasurerail but they were to normally give 90 days written notice of any changes. One of the most important clauses related to the payment of royalties by Pleasurerail to the zoo. These were set on a sliding scale related to the number of passengers carried and are worth quoting in full.

Passengers carried	% of gross receipts from those passengers
First 50,000	nil (but see *)
Second 50,000	2.5%
Third 50,000	5%
Fourth 50,000	10%
Excess over 200,000	15%

(* There shall be paid to ZSL a minimum royalty each year of £250 per annum)

Each year, not later than 31st December, audited accounts were to be submitted to the zoo for the period of the railways operation up to 31st October showing the calculation of the royalty payment. The agreement then defined the procedures for termination, assignment or arbitration if such actions should ever become applicable. With the rails laid, the locomotive situation improving and the paperwork agreed and signed, the railway was now on course for the future.

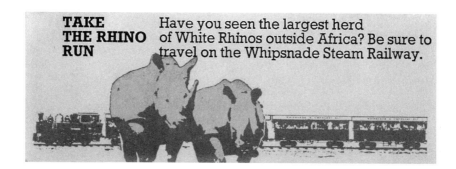

Chapter Five

Consolidation

Line Settles Down Over Full Length

The first manager of the railway, Trevor Barber, left towards the end of 1973. By then the basic pattern of operating had been established and all of the locomotives, to a greater or lesser extent, were operational. Tom Hill remained as the Managing Director of Pleasurerail and the new manager for the railway itself was Mrs Elsie Peach who started in her new job at the end of 1973 or early 1974. Mrs Peach had been working in the children's zoo at Whipsnade and was obviously familiar with the line, the old station being just across the fence, moreover, her husband, Percy, worked at the admission gates. One of the early tasks undertaken by Mrs Peach was to revitalise the range of souvenirs, earlier items apparently having been sold and presumably not re-ordered when Mr Barber left. The range included towels, bookmarks and glasses - everything being railway orientated. There was also an extensive range of postcards, including many depicting steam railways other than Whipsnade. The production of a melamine ashtray which included an embedded photograph caused a memorable incident. In order to take a suitable photograph for use in the production of the ashtray, a train was taken out into the paddock headed by *Excelsior* with Peter Stanbridge at the controls, the idea being that Mrs Peach would pose on the carriage with a rhinoceros in the foreground. The keeper laid down some food pellets and one of the rhinos, called 'Lady', approached. Unfortunately 'Lady' did not simply amble up for the food but entered into a full blown charge at the train, hitting the carriage from which Mrs Peach was supposed to be the impressed onlooker. The charge did not result in any physical damage, but when the dust had settled, Mrs Peach was found hiding underneath the carriage seat, seeking whatever shelter was available! In the end, an appropriate photograph was obtained and the resulting ashtray was very successful, some 6,000 being sold.

At this time there were four permanent staff on the railway. In addition to Mrs Peach, Peter Stanbridge remained in charge of the locomotives assisted by Frank Boatt, and Dick Bennett worked in a general capacity. The permanent staff were supplemented, as has always been the case, by additional seasonal helpers. In the early days under Trevor Barber the railway had been run very much as an enthusiasts' railway as well as being a commercial undertaking. Indeed, Mr Barber's brother, Brian, continued his connection with the railway until about 1975 in this capacity, and after a few years break, was back again to help out towards the end of the decade. With the completion of the circuit, the pattern of operation established and the commercial pressures to achieve repayment of the Pleasurerail investment, the 'feel' of the undertaking began to change and the railway lost some of its earlier 'preservation' character, the enthusiasts which had been so prominent in the early years tending to drift away and move on to other things. The period 1974 to 1979 also saw a fairly rapid turnover of Chief Engineers. After Peter Stanbridge left the railway later in 1974 he was succeeded by Dick Bennett, still assisted by Frank Boatt. The next occupant of the post was Peter Pickering who took over in 1976 and left the following year.

Mrs Peach's grandfather had been an Inspector on the old London Midland & Scottish Railway and she evidently had inherited some 'railway blood', however generally she did not become involved in the mechanical side of operations. On one occasion, however, she decided she would drive a steam-hauled train. The staff were apparently somewhat concerned by this idea, but she completed a circuit, under instruction, and on arriving back at the station strode down the platform, very proud of her achievement, although puzzled as to why there was so much laughter. On looking in a mirror she realised she was covered in dirty spots, the result of the locomotive having primed during her drive! Despite this experience, Mrs Peach clearly retained a great affection for the steam locomotives, only matched by her dislike of *Victor* the diesel.

There had been regular meetings between Tom Hill and the ZSL managers to discuss matters relating to the railway. The Minutes of the meeting on 15th February, 1974 provide a valuable record of the situation on completion of the extension. In Round Close the ditch abutments were still to be faced in brick (the zoo were still complaining that this work was not completed in October 1977 and on to 30th April, 1980!) and work was required to the hand rails around the pond and up to the parapet of the tunnel. Other work outstanding included attention to drainage and the tensioning of wire fences, paint and stain on the loco shed and a smoke baffle for the footbridge, which never does seem to have been fitted, or if it was, it has certainly disappeared now! Under the heading 'New Development' Mr Hill was given agreement to 'proceed with constructing a railway halt on the Valley Meadow side of the rhino paddock, as an experiment for use in the summer season.' A gate was to be made in the paddock fence and 'New signs will be needed to lead visitors to this halt, including signs in the rhino car park area.' This was to become 'Umfolozi Halt' which was duly built by October 1974 just beyond the fence at the end of the rhino paddock. There was another fence, parallel to the rhino fence, which commenced just after the platform of the halt and ran back to the road forming an access some 30 to 40 feet wide along the side of what is now the onager paddock. The halt could serve as an 'escape route' to evacuate passengers if the locomotive should fail, reaching this location not being a problem since the route is downhill all the way from the yard to this point. This second fence has now been removed. The minutes of the meeting seemed to envisage passengers joining or alighting at this point, but this was never actually the case in practice.

The railway fare from Easter 1974 was to be 30p for adults, 20p for children, the adult fare remaining the same as for 1973 but an increase of 5p for children. Party rates were to be 20p for adults and 10p for children. On 8th May, 1974, Tom Hill wrote to Mr C.G.C. Rawlins of the Society expressing his regret over an accident on the railway the previous Sunday. Nobody had been hurt and 'the physical damage was slight.' What appears to have happened is that a carriage broke away from a train which was being reversed from the yard sidings down to the station, the extent of the runaway not being detailed.

Various measures were to be taken to prevent it happening again, among which was the installation of a catch point outside the station limits, just before the footbridge. This remained in place until vacuum braking had been introduced and approved by the Railway Inspectorate in the 1980s. Unfortunately this did not totally resolve the problem. A memo dated 17th February, 1975, from Mr Manton (the Whipsnade curator) informs the ZSL Director of Zoos that,

> for the fourth time we have had a truck 'escape' from the station area on the Pleasurerail Railway this morning. It free-wheeled right through the rhino paddock and came to rest in Big Barn field. Fortunately no damage was caused either to animals or to staff but the 'escape' occurred below the catch points which had been installed to prevent a recurrence of the last accident.

Another problem which took a long time to sort out, and in some respects has never been fully resolved, concerned the access of animals to the tunnel. When it was built, the tunnel allowed animals to move through it between Cut Throat and Round Close paddocks. In June 1974 the zoo had written to Tom Hill expressing their concern about this and Pleasurerail had tried building a grid which was ineffective. The zoo had also been experimenting, with a similar lack of success and Tom Hill suggested trying a new design. The zoo responded on 25th July, 1974 to the effect that they did not believe a grid would work due to the greatly differing sizes of the animals, and suggesting a 'mini-Umfolozi river crossing at one end of the tunnel, probably at the Cut Throat end, it might however, be necessary to do both.' In the meantime a gate had been installed which Pleasurerail staff were supposed to ensure was closed after the last train had passed, needless to say this was occasionally forgotten, leading to complaints from the zoo such as that on 17th March, 1975 drawing attention to the nilgai having moved into the wrong paddock. What is not clear is what prevented this happening during the day between passing trains. The solution adopted by Tom Hill was much as the zoo had suggested and a new ha-ha was built just before the entrance to the tunnel. The construction had not been easy, water flooding into the foundations, but Mr Hill wrote to the zoo on 10th March, 1975 to the effect that the new bridge was complete, although it was not until 29th December, 1975 that he was able to report that work on the Cut Throat side was 'at last' finished. This ha-ha has remained subject to flooding and even now is more akin to a bridge over a pond than a ditch. Although it prevents animals moving between the paddocks, it still allows animals to enter the tunnel from the Round Close end - a situation which will come up again later in the story.

Pleasurerail wrote to the zoo on 29th January, 1975, to notify them that for the 1975 season the fares were to be 40p for adults, 25p for children and a party rate would represent a discount of 20 per cent from those figures. However a further letter dated 18th June, increases the adult fare to 50p, the children's fare remaining at 25p. The railway was suffering some financial difficulties at this time which resulted in the fare increase and a lack of money to spend on the locomotives. A lengthy letter was sent to the zoo by Pleasurerail on 15th October, 1975, proposing several changes in the financial arrangements between the two parties. This letter contains the first suggestion for an 'all in' ticket price, the idea being that on the assumption that the zoo wished to maintain a policy of free attractions within the park, an additional sum should be added to the gate admission price which would cover a trip on the railway. The letter also made an ingenious proposal for a voucher system covering all attractions in lieu of a standard ticket, the idea being to allocate 'values' to each attraction and allowing a measure of customer choice (e.g. animal rides = 1 voucher, childrens zoo = 2, dolphinarium = 2, railway ride = 4). In a further attempt to increase the number of passengers travelling on the railway the letter offered two means by which people may ride without actually paying to enter the park. The first was to have an independent vehicle running between the main gate and the railway, the second being the idea of opening a new separate entrance behind the engine shed giving access directly from the common. Mr Rawlins (the Director of Zoos) responded on 20th November, 1975. He felt it would be a bad time to increase entry prices and could not therefore agree to the combined entry price proposal, and he was not in favour of the voucher system idea either. The scheme for a separate zoo entrance was also rejected, but there was no objection to special parties being escorted from the entrance to the railway and back, provided they made no use of any other park facility, this offer was accepted by Mr Hill on 16th March, 1976. The idea of an all inclusive admission price may have been rejected, but this concept re-appears a number of times as the history of the railway unfolds, ironically it will be seen that on the next occasion it is proposed by the zoo and opposed by Pleasurerail!

During this period Tom Hill took a very leading role in the management of the railway operation, although day to day operating affairs were looked after by Mrs Peach. There were several significant events during her period with the line including a further Royal visit when the railway was host to the Duke and Duchess of Kent, small sized overalls being procured especially in order that their children could be taken for a ride on the footplate, the locomotive involved is believed to have been *Conqueror*. When the railway was first built, the idea had been to provide clear views of the rhinoceros herd. On one occasion, this worth was demonstrated in the most striking manner, when the crew of a train noticed that a rhinoceros was actually in the course of giving birth beside the line as they approached. The train stopped and the passengers were able to witness the event in a way not otherwise possible and many unique photographs were taken. In fact, the train was stopped for so long that there was consternation back at the station that something was wrong. On the return of the train the keeping staff were notified but, unfortunately, the mother prevented them from getting to the calf. Tragically, the newly-born rhino died during the following night, possibly from exposure.

Another major event was the arrival of some very special railway equipment in a snowfall. Over the years of the railway's existence there have been several ideas concerning the display of railway equipment in the form of a museum. For a time, this was being fulfilled by a display of equipment brought over from Africa by the world famous wildlife artist David Shepherd. To describe the Zambezi Sawmills Railway as being full of character and incident would be a considerable understatement. Mr Shepherd first visited this line in 1967 and in

1970 he returned with the BBC to film a short sequence for *The Man Who Loves Giants* which included Mr Shepherd driving one of the ancient steam locomotives. The BBC were so struck by the railway that it was decided to return to Zambia with Mr Shepherd to make a documentary film about the railway. The result was a half hour film called *Last Train to Mulobezi* made in 1973. By now, Mr Shepherd had become the owner of two locomotives and a coach from the railway, locomotive No. 993 and the coach being given to him, and engine No. 156 *Princess of Mulebezi* purchased for a comparatively small sum. After many problems and with the help of numerous friends and contacts, not least being President Kaunda of Zambia, No. 993 and the coach finally arrived back in Britain in March 1975, the other locomotive having been left in Rhodesia (now Zimbabwe) on display at a museum at Bulawayo. On arrival in this country, there was not enough space for the locomotive and coach at the East Somerset Railway with which Mr Shepherd is associated, and Whipsnade agreed to provide a temporary home for the stock which arrived on a Wednesday evening just before Easter in 1975. The film *Last Train to Mulobezi* had just been screened and the BBC filmed the arrival of the stock at Whipsnade in case an alternative ending may be required for a repeat showing.

The siding line on the south side of the platform in the now disused original station platform was relaid to accommodate the 3 ft 6 in. gauge stock. The star exhibit was the large class '7' 4-8-0 locomotive. The engine was built by Sharp, Stewart in Glasgow (works number 4150) in 1896 for the Cape Government Railways in South West Africa. Subsequently, it was taken into the stock of South African Railways, being their No. 993 and eventually purchased for the Zambezi Sawmills Railway in 1971, becoming their No. 390. While at Whipsnade, the engine was returned to full working order and repainted, the colour scheme being black with a light grey smokebox and chimney for many years, later the smokebox and chimney were re-painted black. The engine was accompanied by a tender, loaded with wood, and was put into steam at least once a year and moved up and down the siding. Behind the locomotive was the sizeable bogie coach with end verandas and a clerestory roof painted brown overall with cream sides above the waist. This was Rhodesia Railways sleeping car No. 1808 built in 1927 by Birmingham RC&W Co. Ltd. Inside the coach a photographic display was installed to tell the story of the sawmills railway and the return of the locomotive and coach to Britain. The public could gain access to the coach from the old station platform with the aid of wooden steps up to the veranda ends of the coach.

The film *Last Train to Mulobezi* had also featured a Ford Prefect which was used as an inspection trolley on the sawmills railway. The original had fallen apart in Africa after filming was finished but Mr Shepherd had the idea of finding a similar car and adding it to the display at Whipsnade. The Ford Motor Company at Dagenham found a suitable 1938 Ford Prefect which they donated and which was then renovated by Mercedes Great Britain. The body was mounted on flanged wheels by the Royal Engineers and the vehicle was added to the display in front of the locomotive. The bodywork looked immaculate and was painted medium blue and had all the appearance of a normal, if elderly, car sitting on rails. In fact, it was in running order and was occasionally driven up and down the display track. In 1976, a ceremony took place when the car was 'officially' handed over by Sir Terence Beckett, then Chairman of Ford, and the guests included the Zambian High Commissioner. As Mr Shepherd said in his book *A Brush with Steam* (the source of much of this information, alas now out of print) this seemed particularly appropriate since President Kaunda had referred to this part of Whipsnade as 'a little part of Zambia'.

The accuracy of this impression was reinforced by the construction of Mulobezi Halt to complete the display area. This was located just past the road crossing between the main line and the old station area where the Zambezi stock was located, the name being derived from the sawmills railway which connected Livingstone with the sawmill township of Mulobezi. The top of the grass bank was levelled off and covered with concrete and a platform, probably constructed from sleepers, was built up by the main line almost back to the road. There was a large station signboard announcing the name of the halt, a station seat, a small garden shed in natural dark wood preservative colour and the area was surrounded by white painted fencing behind the platform and across the top of the bank, from where steps led down to the Zambezi display. The halt was certainly present by October 1975 and had probably been in use earlier in the summer of that year, and it had become disused by June 1983, quite possibly earlier. In the meantime, the East Somerset Railway had been negotiating to acquire additional land for its site at Cranmore and by early 1990, preparations were being made for the movement of the display items. On 29th June, 1990, a chart for the required sequence of movements of the locomotive, coach and tender was supplied to the haulier, together with a note that the 3 ft 6 in. gauge track would be disconnected into lengths of not more than 40 ft and could be moved at the same time as the stock. In October 1990 the Zambezi stock was removed to its permanent home at Cranmore. There is now little evidence of the halt, the sleepers which formed the front face of the platform are visible but in a poor state. The concrete on top of the bank is still there, as are the steps which led down to the old platform and display area. All the fencing on top of the bank which used to surround the area has been removed, together with the station sign, wooden hut and seat. Thus, it may be argued that the Whipsnade Railway has had four stations in its life, two of which have been closed and another not actually used by passengers!

During the period 1974 to 1977 the locomotives were steadily re-painted into a variety of colours with *Superior*, *Conqueror* and *Victor* all acquiring new paint schemes (described in Chapter Eight under each locomotive). *Excelsior* had also received her new colours after the rebuild of 1972/73 and this left only *Chevallier* in her original colours, although for most of this time the locomotive was dismantled and out of use. Thus, from a collection of all green locomotives, the railway now had every engine in a different colour. The operating practices changed as well, for locomotives are known to have been worked during this time with only one person on the footplate. In fact weekday operations are said to have been run by just two staff, one selling tickets and the other working the train. Graeme Carr was one of the drivers by 1975, and thinking back on it, admits that it was remarkable that an 18 or 19 year-old was entrusted with driving a locomotive such as *Conqueror* single handed! Another young driver recalls the sheer exhaustion which followed weekday turns of one man operation during the school holidays which would start with lighting up at about 8.00 am followed by cleaning, oiling and coaling the locomotive, sweeping the coaches and platform forecourt, running trains from 10.30 am to 5.00 pm, return the locomotive to the shed, drop the fire, clean the ashpan and fill the boiler, only then to close up and go home.

The circuit was now established as being driven clockwise and from a driving point of view there was no particular problem, the fire was built up before starting and by the time the downhill section on the approach to the rhino paddock was reached the locomotive was blowing off. Plenty of steam remained for the climb back up through the tunnel and round to the station again where the fire could be attended to. During this period the locomotives were progressively turn in order that they all faced in the same direction, uphill out of Whipsnade Central. *Excelsior* was apparently turned during the winter of 1973/74, the method being as simple as lifting her with a 20 ton crane, swinging her round, and then back down again. *Conqueror* seems to have been turned in the following winter (1975/76) but the precise method has not been determined, *Superior* was also definitely facing in the new direction by 1975. The trains did have, or should have had, a guard and relied on hand brakes, there being no vacuum brakes at this time. The problem was one of safety and a story is told by staff who knew the railway at that time that in 1976 a driver actually fell asleep while working *Excelsior* and fell off the engine during one trip. It has been impossible to check the accuracy of this story, but the next on-site Manager to be appointed had certainly heard of it and rapidly re-introduced two-person working on the footplate on taking over for the 1978 season.

Unfortunately, no passenger figures have been found for the years prior to 1976, but in the 1976/77 season the railway carried around 103,000 passengers, this being nearly 25 per cent of visitors to the zoo. The fares which were to come into effect on 8th April, 1977 for the new season were 50p for adults and 30p for children. Clearly, the railway was establishing itself as a significant attraction in the park, but it also seems to have become rather run down, perhaps as a result of carrying such large numbers of passengers, although there also seems to have been a shortage of money during the previous few years, and a shortage of staff to carry out maintenance and repairs.

The start of 1978 saw further changes in the railway staff. Elsie Peach had left in the previous November and moved to Hastings with her husband where they were to run the miniature railway owned by Tom Hill. Her replacement was Mrs Pauline Haines, who had worked on the platform side of operations at Whipsnade Central during the previous year, and started as manager in time for the 1978 season. Peter Pickering also left towards the end of 1977 and was succeeded by Rod McLeod who, it may be recalled had begun his association with the railway on an occasional and part time basis back in February 1971. He took up the full time post of Chief Engineer in March 1978, about the same time as Pauline Haines. During April and May 1978 there were occasions when no train was run because there were insufficient people in the park to justify operating. This led to complaints, and the response from Pleasurerail that the problem was increasing costs and decreasing attendance, but they said a sign was put up at the station and in future they would put one by the zoo gate when services were curtailed. The fares for this year were 60p for adults and 30p for children. In the event, the railway carried over 106,000 passengers in the year, which represented an even higher percentage of zoo visitors than the previous year at 26.5 per cent. There was also a slightly unusual complaint by the zoo in 1978. The problem was that on 7th November, 1978, a delivery had arrived for Pleasurerail 'long after the park had closed to the public' without prior notice to the zoo. The delivery was 'a small steam engine'. It seems that this must have been the Knebworth engine *Sezela*, since is known that in early 1979 (apparently around May or a little earlier) there had been a break-in at the shed area and among the items stolen were pipes and fittings from this engine. The average tenure of about two years for the Chief Engineers continued, Rod McLeod finally leaving the railway in December 1979. The new Chief Engineer was to be Pauline Haines' husband Peter, who had been helping out on a part time basis during Rod McLeod's tenure, and commenced in the full time post on 1st January, 1980. When Peter was appointed, they were the only full time staff on the railway. The first job for Peter Haines was to provide the motive power for the following season since, on his arrival, nothing was in working condition at all. *Excelsior*, which had been used continuously since her major rebuild, was stripped down awaiting a boiler inspection, *Conqueror* was in need of new boiler tubes, although the engine had been working during the previous year. *Superior* was outside the shed partly in pieces, *Chevallier* was inside the shed largely stripped, without a cab or tanks and even *Victor* had blown head gaskets and was not working. *Hector* was derelict, never having been touched since it arrived at the railway. *Excelsior* and *Victor* were fairly easily sorted out and were ready to operate traffic for the new season. The next locomotive to be returned to service was *Conqueror* which was ready for the following season.

Following her lengthy boiler overhaul *Chevallier* was the next locomotive to return to service. It will be recalled that in the very early days *Chevallier* had caused some alarm when being returned to service after repairs to her regulator. The great day for steaming her after re-assembly threatened to be a repeat occasion, for as steam was being raised the engine showed no sign of working. Amidst some consternation and discussion as to what could be wrong, there was a sudden loud 'plop' as a wad of cotton waste which had been stuffed into the blast pipe and forgotten about came loose and was blown about fifty feet into the air!

The Whipsnade Railway has a perfect safety record in relation to its passengers, but it may now be revealed that it came perilously close to disaster during the second visit by Royalty! The railway was to be visited on Saturday 23rd May, 1981, when the Duke of Edinburgh came to Whipsnade to launch the celebrations of the park's fiftieth anniversary, the Duke himself having been President of the Zoological Society of London between 1960 and 1977. As when Princess Margaret visited the railway eight years earlier, everything was spruced up for the event and the Royal train, headed by *Excelsior* under the charge of Peter Haines, waited in the platform for the Royal party. There had been some delay in the proceedings and the Duke was behind schedule, what was not apparent was that Mr Haines was growing increasingly concerned because of an injector failure on *Excelsior*. By the time the Royal party was aboard the train the glass was already showing the water level to be worryingly low and by the time the train had completed the climb to the yard and started the downhill run into the paddock *Excelsior* had a good fire, was blowing off steam - and had virtually no water. Fortunately the trip was completed safely and as soon as *Excelsior* arrived back at Whipsnade Central the fire was dropped and disaster averted.

The railway has also entertained many other celebrities, including Johnny Morris, who filmed a spot for *Animal Magic* and Tommy Steele, for whom Whipsnade Central signal box served as a changing room while filming in the park. In 1983, the railway provided a special train for a video shot by Kyodo Television of Tokyo, which provided some useful additional income. In November 1987, the railway received a small sum as a token of appreciation from the BBC Bristol Production Centre for providing a special train for filming in connection with the programme *Zoo Week*.

A joint inspection of the railway by Major Jeremy Monson (for Linehaul/Pleasurerail) and Mr J. Toovey (ZSL) took place on 23rd April, 1982. A broad range of largely detail matters were noted for action, mostly by the railway! Among the more significant were that Linehaul were to arrange for the automatic arm and related equipment at the road crossing to be overhauled and renewed where necessary, a yellow box was also to be painted in the road and 'unmanned crossing' signs erected. A considerable amount of work on fencing was required, and the railway were to replace broken and rotting sleepers 'particularly along the track beside the bactrian camel paddock. They may decide to widen the bend here in due course, to improve safety and working.' It was also agreed to dispense with the 'Umfolozi River' signs. A slightly strange minute notes 'Linehaul Ltd hope to be able to roof over the open cutting beside the road bridge in due course.' This obviously refers to the first part of the 'tunnel' before the actual road bridge - but why would it be beneficial to roof over the remainder? Since animals could move through the tunnel one would have thought the reduction in natural light and added accumulation of steam and smoke in the enclosed space would have caused more problems than already existed. In any event, this work was never carried out. Various letters had been exchanged concerning royalty payments and on 4th December, 1982, Linehaul supplied figures for the previous three years which were:

	1980	1981	1982
Takings	£61,077-80	£63,190-00	£64,135-50
Passengers	98,852	102,771	87,306

The year 1982 also saw attention turn to *Superior*, which was still rotting away outside the shed. The railway were particularly anxious to have *Superior* working. *Excelsior* was reliable but could not handle full length trains, *Conqueror* had more than enough power but was an inconvenient and uneconomical locomotive to operate, and *Chevallier* was also rather large for the railway. In November 1982, *Superior* was sent away to Steamtown at Carnforth in Lancashire in the expectation that she would be away for about 18 months.

There seem to have been some initial delays in getting work moving but by June 1983 Steamtown were reporting they were 'shortly to make a concerted effort' and by January 1984 there had been 'considerable progress'. Things did not apparently progress so well and the anticipated 18 months came and went. It was not until the middle of June 1985 that the Whipsnade people went up to Steamtown, anticipating inspection of the completed locomotive, only to find that it was still not finished. During the time *Superior* had been away services were operated by *Excelsior*, supplemented by *Victor* on busy days, the decision having been made to stop using *Conqueror* at the end of 1983. Although *Chevallier* was in a workable condition there was pressure on the manageress to get the railway into a profitable state and the use of this engine was not worthwhile in relation to the cost of coal, etc. The situation was clearly causing much concern to Mrs Haines, who complained that as a result of *Superior* not having been returned the railway was losing passengers and disappointing others who had expected to travel behind a steam engine. In July 1985, *Superior* returned to Whipsnade, but the saga was far from over. A long list of faults were found on her and, to cap it all, the whistle blew continuously as soon as steam was raised! This particular problem seems to have been resolved by fitting the whistle from *Conqueror*. By August, Mrs Haines was not happy about the situation, but felt there was no option but to use *Superior* since *Excelsior* could not cope at that time of the year. The strain was obviously considerable, since on 22nd July she had written to Mr McAlpine, who was also the Chairman and majority shareholder of Steamtown, expressing disgust at the condition of *Superior* on its return after two years and eight months of work. The letter continued with references to the upheavals in the zoo, a lack of information from the Zoological Society of London, and all boiled over with the comment '....only thing absolutely sure of is imminent demise of the Whipsnade & Umfolozi Railway as we know it'. The letter was noted as having been written at 11.00 pm and it had obviously been a very bad day!

The problems continued, with Pleasurerail staff working on the locomotive as well as visits to Whipsnade by Steamtown fitters in an effort to resolve the outstanding issues. By 15th January, 1986, Steamtown wrote to the railway confirming they had been instructed to rectify the vacuum brake system recently fitted, and when done '...this will complete our work on *Superior* as far as I can see'. Whipsnade did not agree, Mrs Haines' reply on 18th January summing up the railway's feelings with the comment about the completion of the work '...must be joking!' The letter then detailed remaining faults which included: play in the valve gear, vacuum brake not working, a creaking noise from the offside valve gear, lubricator tubes fouling the vacuum cylinder frame, and several more. In the end, all the problems were resolved and *Superior* was ready for the 1987 season. The correspondence finally tailed off in July 1987 after Mrs Haines had delivered some rather caustic comments in defence of Pleasurerail staff to Steamtown!

With the return of *Superior* with vacuum braking it was then possible to undertake the work to equip *Excelsior* as well. Fitting vacuum brakes would greatly improve the safety of the railway and do away with the need for the driver to bring the train to a stand and then hop off the footplate to pull on the carriage brakes when working single handed, a practice which had to be performed in Round Close if nobody was available to open the Crossing Gates in advance of arrival! An incident which demonstrated the weakness of relying on the single screw-braked carriage occurred with *Hector* on 26th June, 1986. By this time *Hector* had been renovated and was working, but the wheels were in a poor state and the springing was unbalanced, with the result that the locomotive left the track all too easily. On one occasion as the train came up through the tunnel, the spring on the front near side wheel broke and *Hector* left the rails and lurched sideways, the buffer beam hitting the side of the tunnel. The marks are still visible on the left side of the wall where *Hector* came to rest. The first task in any such incident is to get the passengers to safety. In this situation the problem was compounded, because behind the train was the water-filled ha-ha, and *Hector* was blocking the tunnel at the front. The passengers had to be unloaded from the train and each pass through the cab of the locomotive in order to reach Round Close. Fortunately, the paddock was only occupied by deer and llama so passengers were not in any danger from the animals as they walked the remainder of the circuit, including down the ditch and up the other side at the last ha-ha before the Central Avenue crossing. Remarkably, not one passenger took up the offer of a refund, in fact when Mrs Haines notified the Railway Inspectorate of the incident she was able to refer to the passenger reaction as being 'Big joke, livened up their day'! The story does not end here. The next task was to get *Hector* back on to the rails, so Peter Haines who was driving screwed down the hand brake on the front coach and uncoupled the train from the locomotive. The slope becomes quite steep from the approach to the tunnel and through Round Close and the single hand brake was not up to the task of holding the train. The coaches then set off on their own back into the paddock and did not come to rest until reaching the rhino paddock - from the reverse direction!

Back in April 1983 Mr Rawlins had written to Sir William McAlpine reminding him that he had mentioned some time before that it would be possible to equip trains with a loudspeaker system. The zoo were prepared to provide staff, or volunteers, to give a running commentary 'this summer.' This was not a new idea, such a commentary had been introduced some years before but various problems had arisen which included the level of volume required resulting in complaints from residents outside the park, the difficulty in finding commentators and various other technical problems, these all resulting in the idea being dropped. The railway still had the equipment and was prepared to try again with one set of coaches, the idea being to fit the equipment to each coach as it received its new roof. Unfortunately there were problems with the new roofs and by August Mrs Haines had to inform the zoo that it would not be possible to introduce commentaries in 1983. In due course, the equipment was fitted and train commentaries remain a feature on the railway at busy times. The commentary is provided by a zoo volunteer and there are further details in Chapter Seven.

From Africa to Asia

While the railway remained in its existing physical location, the mid-1980s saw a transformation for the line between the continents of Africa and Asia. There was another break with the past when Tom Hill moved on in his professional career and was no longer able to retain involvement with the railway, ceasing to be Managing Director of Pleasurerail and selling his shareholding to Sir William McAlpine. Looking back on his involvement, Mr Hill refers to it as having been 'a labour of love', an echo of the statement, 'I loved it' made by Mrs Peach recalling her time at the railway and a sentiment encountered repeatedly when talking with people who have been involved with the line. In early 1984, the zoo were considering alterations to the display of the animals in the park, the main objective being to bring the animals closer to the visitors, both in relation to the roads in the park and the railway. This was also to involve alterations to the rhino paddock. All of these changes were coupled to at least some degree with the financial situation of the Society and the whole period was one of uncertainty for all concerned.   Part of the zoo proposals included incorporating a railway ride within the admission price for the park and paying a percentage to Pleasurerail thus, in effect, the railway would become a 'free' ride for visitors. There was also a proposal to extend the railway in conjunction with the proposed alterations to the animal paddocks. The idea of an 'all in' admission price was not of course new, Tom Hill had suggested it back in October 1975 but at that time the zoo were not in favour of the idea. The situation now was somewhat different and the biggest concern for Mrs Haines was the cost of providing the railway with sufficient additional locomotives, carriages and a signalling/communication system to cope with the increased traffic. In addition what if, having done so, the zoo were unable to bring all their plans to fruition, leaving Pleasurerail 'up the proverbial creek with the bank owning both paddles' as Mrs Haines put it in her letter of 2nd September, 1984 to Sir William McAlpine. The Pleasurerail Directors were not happy with the proposals either but decided to wait until something more definite was received from the zoo, at which time they would discuss it further. It will be recalled from the earlier episode with *Superior* that this period was causing a great deal of strain for the railway staff, with considerable uncertainty about the future of both zoo and railway. It also has to be said that in the early 1980s relations between the railway and zoo had been getting a bit strained in some respects, incidents such as that which occurred on Sunday 4th September, 1983, did not help. Mrs Haines had been off work sick and the young assistant left in charge became confused as to which day it was. Thinking it was a Saturday, she had closed the railway early and this only came to light when Mrs Haines subsequently asked if she had done the payroll and summary sheets. Shortly after, Major Monson and Mr Rawlins met for lunch and things were smoothed over!

The years 1983 and 1984 were busy in other ways involving work on developments which did not come out despite the planning. The railway never had, and still does not have, any covered accommodation for its carriage stock. Plans were drawn up in March 1983 for an extension to be erected on the east side of the engine shed to form a carriage shed. The building would have been constructed in much the same way as the shed, with horizontal tongue and groove boarding on a timber frame fixed to a steel frame. The extension would not have reached the full length of the existing shed. Discussions over the design dragged on for a long time and a meeting, held on 30th August, 1984, resolved some issues but raised new ones, such as adding a new bay to the existing shed and taking the carriage shed extension back to the new end of the shed, and installing roller front doors to the loco shed. The representative of the Zoological Society at this meeting then outlined the importance of the railway in the Zoo Development Plan if its proposals were implemented. The railway would then become the main viewing and transport system for the zoo and the new exhibits adjoining would be designed with that in mind. 'Clearly, this would mean the whole railway installation has to be upgraded' read the record of the meeting. Mrs Haines had been accompanied to the meeting by Major Monson who said that this possibility 'put a new complexion on things and would require investment; the original investment had only just been paid off.' Mrs Haines expressed the same concerns as she had before; at present the line could just cope with 3,000 visitors a day, roughly 25 per cent of those visiting the park. The new proposals would mean more than double the numbers would need to be carried and she felt the railway could not cope if the ride were to be free. There would need to be investment in signals, trains would be longer, requiring station platforms to be extended and many other improvements. Considerable work went into costing the many improvements and upgrades required to meet the various plans at this time, the total coming to over £238,000. A meeting with a zoo official in September 1984 brought up yet another idea, this time for a second station in the rhino paddock to serve a tea shop. The first ideas seem to have anticipated about 75 passengers arriving and departing every ten minutes and would have involved building a branch off the main line. The location of the proposed cafe is not at all clear, further details appear later under the heading 'Plans That Never Happened'.

The Pleasurerail Directors met and following their discussions Mr W.J. Germing wrote a detailed letter to David Jones, the new Director of Zoos, on 4th October, 1984, setting out the position from the railway's point of view. The Directors recognised that the proposals for re-organising the zoo could result in banning cars from the park and that all transport would therefore be handled by the 'Road Train' and the railway. The improvements, including building a new station by the 'waterhole', had been costed and it was anticipated that fresh capital investment of £140,000 would be required - some of the work and figures had obviously been revised from the earlier estimate. In addition, the annual running expenses of the railway would increase because of the extra staff required and funding of capital expenditure by way of depreciation. The letter confirmed that Pleasurerail did not have the capital resources to meet the anticipated expenditure, moreover, although they had discussed the possibility of seeking an interest free loan from ZSL, they were unwilling to enter into further borrowing. The railway had been built originally by using funds borrowed to provide the necessary capital and the companies resources had been committed to repaying the loans. The original investment had taken considerably longer to clear than had originally been anticipated. Pleasurerail had only become free of debt two years earlier, and since the railway was now basically profitable as it stood, the Directors were not minded to undertake further large investments which would, in effect, put them back where they started. The Pleasurerail Directors had considered the possibility of the ZSL financing the extensions and improvements, but since the assets supplied by the railway and the zoo would inevitably become mixed they did not consider this to be a practical arrangement. The conclusion reached was contained in the last paragraph of the letter; the directors had concluded that to enable the Society to extend the railway in accordance with its plans, ZSL could purchase Pleasurerail, thus bringing the railway entirely under the control of the Society. The cost of replacing the railway, including all rolling stock and equipment, at 1984 prices was estimated to be £500,000, but the directors were prepared to accept £225,000. By purchasing the railway for this sum, and carrying out the proposed improvements, for a total expenditure of £365,000 the Society would have a 'Railway fit for its future role in the transport service of Whipsnade Park'.

Not surprisingly, the Society took some time to consider the situation, the proposal being circulated among senior ZSL staff. An internal zoo memo in November 1984 shows that Victor Manton was in favour of a purchase of the railway, but the decision from the Society finally came in a letter from David Jones dated 17th January, 1985. The Society had now received agreement from the Department of the Environment to provide sufficient funds to cover the annual deficit, but had not made any specific allocation for capital investment, although there was a commitment to match funds raised by the Society up to a ceiling. Although ZSL had some capital resulting from consultancy work to spend on Whipsnade, the pressing need was to ensure the infrastructure of the park was more efficiently organised and run. The 'bottom line' was, 'I cannot therefore see us being able to raise a sufficient sum of money in the near future to buy the railway.' The letter ended by reference to a forthcoming discussion with Sir William when Mr Jones planned to suggest that the railway should continue to operate 'in the same way as we have done successfully for the past few years.' Mr Germing replied on 24th January noting that there would not be sufficient capital to purchase the railway, and confirming that Pleasurerail were not actually looking to sell, but had felt such a course was the only practical method by which the zoo's apparent plans would be achieved. The letter closed 'We shall of course co-operate in every way, as far as we are able so to do, in making sure the railway at Whipsnade is run so as to fit in with the Zoological Society's requirements.' The idea of the zoo purchasing the railway did not go any further for the time being, although as we shall see, it was to be revived a few years later.

In the event, of course, the idea of extending the railway also came to nothing (see 'Plans That Never Happened' for further detail), nor, indeed, the building of a carriage shed, although both ideas saw a revival in the 1990s. In 1985 however, the zoo had made the decision to re-arrange the animal displays to bring animals of the same continents together into logical geographic collections. The Africa region was to be on the western side of the park near the

Downs. The rhinos seem to have been due to move to their new location in 1985 with the Whipsnade & Umfolozi title for the railway thus becoming redundant. Despite the earlier considerations of extensions and changes to the paddocks, by February 1986 no decision had been made on a new name and Mrs Haines had to suggest that the existing name remain in use for the forthcoming season. On 10th February, 1986 the zoo wrote to Mrs Haines and gave a list of the animals which would be located in the paddocks surrounding the railway and noted that for the time being the line would be referred to in publicity handouts as the 'Asian Railway'. They hoped that the Pleasurerail Directors would soon be able to select an attractive name for the railway which could be used for publicity purposes. The name eventually arrived at was the 'Great Whipsnade Railway' which, of course, incorporated the initials of a somewhat larger GWR concern of the past and allowed a name which would not become dated again in the event of the animals, or indeed route of the line, being changed in the future. In view of the above, it is strange that according to the zoo's animal movements records, the rhinos actually moved to Spicers field in January 1987. Possibly the move was delayed for some reason and in the event the Railway changed its name prematurely!

The fares for 1985 were now increased to £1.20 for adults (80p in a party) and 60p for children (40p in a party) and the figures supplied in connection with royalty payments were:

	1985	1986
Takings	£79,437-80	£83,311-00
Passengers	88,633	91,477

By virtue of its location, the fortunes of the railway are inevitably linked to those of the zoo itself and with Whipsnade having the status of the 'Country Home' of the Zoological Society of London, with the flagship zoo at Regents Park, inevitably Whipsnade was affected by events elsewhere. By 1984, the Zoological Society of London was in deep financial difficulties. To compound the problems for Whipsnade, the park had seen a fall in attendance in the 1984/85 season of nearly 28,000 visitors from the 1983/84 season and money was very short. The figures for the following season were even worse with a further drop although, oddly, the number of passengers travelling on the railway actually showed an increase. The 1986/87 season, however, was encouraging for the park with an eventual healthy increase in visitors to the highest level since 1980/81. The worrying fact was that the number of passengers travelling on the railway fell alarmingly to the lowest point for at least a decade, 84,121, which represented just 22 per cent of visitors to the park. Against the background of uncertainty surrounding both the park and the railway already outlined, it comes as little surprise that the Pleasurerail Directors were reluctant to incur any unnecessary expenditure. Valuable insights to the condition of the railway and the method of operating at this mid-point in the railway's existence are provided by two reports by the Railway Inspectorate in 1986.

The first inspection took place on 18th August, 1986 and the report was made by L. Abbott of the Inspectorate on 4th September, 1986. Mr Abbott had been accompanied by Mr and Mrs Haines, the only two full time employees at this point, and commences with a general description of the railway with the various features of the circuit being defined by reference to a notional clock face, e.g. Whipsnade Central being located at the 9 o'clock position. A most interesting observation was made concerning the weight of rail used since this has often been the source of conflicting descriptions, official or otherwise. The rails were noted as having been laid in two stages, stage 1 of one mile being laid in 85 lb. per yard flat bottom rail, and stage 2 also of one mile in 65 lb. per yard flat bottom rail. The inspector was clearly very concerned about the track, this section commencing with the words 'The condition of the track indicates a total lack of preventive maintenance. It is rapidly deteriorating and must receive immediate attention to the following'. The inspector then reported that he had pointed out which sections needed complete re-sleepering and others where spot re-sleepering was necessary. Mr Abbott felt that almost the whole length of the line required lifting, packing and slewing to get it into correct horizontal and vertical alignment. As if this were not enough, the inspector found very few expansion gaps between rails and foresaw severe buckling in hot weather, and found several sections of the track which were short of ballast or where it required building up on the shoulders. All of the fishplates 'must be removed and greased' and a number of rail ends which had been burnt off by an oxy-acetylene flame were noted - this practice not being permitted 'as it leads to fatigue fractures.' Under 'Rules and Regulations' the inspector found that the minimum age for drivers before being allowed to drive unaccompanied was 16 years, and the minimum age of staff allowed to work on the railway had been raised from 14 to 15 years. 'This practice must cease immediately' was the response - the inspector requiring that drivers be a minimum of 21 years-old, and guards at least 18 years of age. There follows a factual outline of the locomotives and passenger stock and the observation that the fitting of continuous vacuum brakes was long overdue. After the criticism of the track it almost comes as a surprise that the conclusion was that the operation of the railway 'would appear satisfactory', subject to attention being given to a number of items!

The report of the inspection must however have caused some alarm in several circles, certainly on 8th September, 1986 the Department of Transport wrote to Sir William McAlpine and included the words;

I feel that you ought to see a copy of the report yourself as it reveals a considerable amount of things which to put it mildly leave much to be desired. In particular, on the track side, there is a lot of work to be done and I am sure that a gentle push by you would not go amiss.

The Pleasurerail Directors clearly reacted with little delay and on 6th November, 1986 a further inspection took place at the railway at the request of Major the Hon. J Monson. This time the inspector was Mr W.J. May of the Railway Inspectorate who prepared his report on 27th November.

In addition to Mr May and Major Monson, the inspection was also attended by Mr G. Hinchcliffe (appointed as Honorary Engineer for Pleasurerail Ltd in early 1986), Mrs P.R. Haines (manageress, Pleasurerail), Mr P. Haines (now described as fitter/loco driver, Pleasurerail), Mr Bush (Hocking Ltd) and Major P.M. Olver (Railway Inspectorate). It may reasonably be surmised that the presence of additional personnel representing Pleasurerail was connected with a recognition of the problems and the intention to correct them, the people who would be responsible for executing the work being present to see and discuss first hand with the inspector the remedial action required. The condition of the track, not surprisingly, again came in for particular attention. In fact, the general standard of track maintenance was bluntly described as not good, with a recommendation that considerably more attention should be given to it in the close season than had been in the past. Whilst it was acknowledged that the relatively heavy rails of 65 lb. and 75 lb. per yard meant that the odd bad sleeper was not as significant as it would be with lighter track, a number of sleepers were found to have come to the end of their useful life. The track was described as requiring lining and levelling throughout its length with additional ballast necessary at a number of locations. It seems that in the past there had been problems with thermal buckling and it was stated that fishplates and bolts must be removed, greased and reassembled before the next operating season and thereafter annually, and all missing and loose fishplate bolts were to be replaced and tightened. The section through the 'rhino paddock', laid some 16 years before, came in for special criticism. The sleepers were described as so deteriorated as to have become unserviceable, the trackbed as sub-standard, and the track itself as having become displaced off its original line by buckling. While the original rails were accepted as probably capable of re-use, Mr May declared that if the railway was to continue in operation, the whole section was to be completely relaid on a reconstructed bed before the start of the 1988 season. The drainage under the 'road over rail bridge' (note - the tunnel) was described as unsatisfactory, resulting in mud mixing with the remains of the ballast, and soakaway drains were recommended. One particular turnout, unfortunately not clearly identified, was completely condemned, public services not being allowed until missing and loose bolts in the heel blocks had been properly installed. A further requirement was that the weighted operating levers on all turnouts should be mounted on timbers integral with the track. The section of the report on track and structures is rounded off by confirming that the facing points in the round paddock (note - Round Close paddock which includes Daedalus Lake) may continue to be clipped and padlocked while only one platform was in use at Whipsnade Central. The reference to this point confirms that the railway was still normally operated in a clockwise direction, the pattern which has remained to date. If it became necessary to work trains from both platforms then a two lever ground frame with facing points locking lever released by an Annetts type key should be provided. The only comment on structures as such concerned the wall of the outer platform at Whipsnade Central station which was bowed, presumably due to hydrostatic pressure. The situation required monitoring and if it showed significant cracking or fear of collapse the platform must be closed to the public until it had been repaired.

The report goes on to provide some detail of staffing and Major Monson raised two points of some significance to the operation of the railway for the future. At that time the railway had two full-time staff supplemented, as always, for the high season by temporary staff who tended to be students seeking work for the vacation period. Major Monson made the point that, as a result, the railway enjoyed the advantage of an intelligent and reliable group of seasonal staff who would accept discipline, a situation not necessarily enjoyed by other minor railways reliant on volunteers. No doubt some of the other railways would have a response of their own (!) but, in the context, Major Monson was making a valid point in relation to the staff recruited at Whipsnade. The difficulty was finding enough people over 21 years-old to act as locomotive drivers. The request was therefore made for a relaxation of the requirement contained in the HSE guidance note PM18 regarding the minimum age for drivers. The appeal was evidently made well, for agreement was given that until further notice Whipsnade was allowed to use drivers and trainee drivers of 18 years or more and other operating staff such as firemen, guards and signalmen may work alone provided they were 18, and people of between 16 and 18 could work in these jobs provided they were under the direct supervision of fully qualified staff. It was also agreed that all operational staff should be passed out on practical operating aspects, emergency procedures and rules by independent and qualified supervisors or railway officers. The second point raised by Major Monson also provides an insight to the method of actually operating trains on the railway, and demonstrates that two-person working had been re-introduced since the inspector was asked whether single person working would be permitted. The request was turned down and the point was made that on steam-hauled trains the second person must act as a fireman on the locomotive. On diesel-hauled trains, however, the second person may either ride in the cab or as a guard in a passenger vehicle. In both cases the second person was expected to maintain a watch on the train and warn the driver of 'anything untoward occurring.'

Since the railway had first opened, the braking arrangements consisted solely of the locomotive brakes together with the manually applied brakes on the coaches. An attempt had been made by Trevor Barber around 1972 to devise a continuous steam brake, but the experiment had been a failure. At the time of the 1986 inspections, trains still did not have automatically applied brakes although it was planned to adopt vacuum braking in the following year. The Railway Inspectorate wanted to witness a test which would demonstrate that a single braked vehicle would be able to hold itself together with an unbraked vehicle when fully loaded on the maximum gradient on the line. Provided the tests were satisfactory, approval would be given to remove the catch points in advance of the station. The plan was to fit vacuum brakes to at least two out of three, or three out of four, passenger carriages and to all locomotives.

One coach was already at Steamtown, Carnforth, in early 1986 to be fitted with a vacuum brake system and was to be returned to Whipsnade for testing. If the installation proved satisfactory, the other coaches would be dealt with at Whipsnade. In the event, the fitting of vacuum brakes was done in two stages. The greater part of the work was completed in 1987/88, but the remainder of the installations were not finished until 1992.

The inspection to test the vacuum brakes was made on 2nd April, 1987, by Mr W.J. May of the Railway Inspectorate. By now *Excelsior* had been fitted with a steam ejector, vacuum brake operating valve and duplex vacuum gauges, although its own braking system remained independent and unchanged with a steam brake and hand brake on the driving wheels. Three carriages had also been fully fitted and a fourth piped. The test took place with *Excelsior* and the four carriages, the piped one being coupled to the locomotive. The actual tests were carried out by reversing the train at about 8 mph down a gradient, closing the regulator and making an emergency application of the vacuum brake. By successively disconnecting the hoses between the vehicles and repeating the tests the effect of braking by three, two and one vehicles was ascertained. With three braked vehicles the stopping distance was 20 feet, with two it was 30 feet and with one it was 45 feet. The tests were satisfactory and it was agreed that up to two un-braked vehicles but through piped vehicles may be worked with three braked vehicles, or one un-braked with two braked vehicles. The un-braked, but piped, vehicles were always to be marshalled next to the locomotive. Also in attendance at this visit was Mr L. Bush, a director of J. Bush & Sons Ltd who had carried out remedial work on the track after the previous inspection. The work they had done was considered to be of a good standard, although to reduce expense many of the sleeper beds were unfilled, the work to be done by volunteers. Considerable work had been done to the track, including removal and lubrication of fishplates, rail gaps re-established and 'several sections which were wide to gauge corrected.' Long timbers had also been provided at all point lever positions. The drain gulleys in the tunnel had been cleared but the inspector was still concerned that the animals were churning up the embankment and causing mud to flow into the cutting and suggested that the wing wall for the bridge should be extended to act as a retainer. Subject to some outstanding items from the previous report the inspector recommended approval for the continued operation of the railway. This series of reports comes to an encouraging conclusion with a letter dated 24th April, 1987, from the Department of Transport to Major Monson which enclosed a copy of the 2nd April report by Mr May. The words which must have come as a relief were: 'Your winter's endeavours appear to have paid dividends and providing the sleeper beds are re-filled as a matter of urgency the track and rolling stock now appear to be in reasonably good heart.'

The period under the management of Mrs Haines and her husband was a tough one with long hours and discussions on railway problems late into the evening. The railway had achieved profitability, the locomotive situation was much improved from when they started and passengers were carried in greater safety and comfort following the introduction of vacuum braking and new carriage roofing. Mrs Haines had decided to retire at the end of the season and her report to the Directors written in November 1988 was to be her last.

The railway had carried 94,754 passengers in the 1987/88 season, the highest total since 1980/81. This figure would largely be the result of the zoo attendance being over 400,000 for the year, the highest since 1976/77. Mrs Haines suggested that consideration might be given to an increase in fares, along with an increase in staff salaries. There was still considerable doubt surrounding the future and hints that consideration was being given to a takeover of the railway by the zoo. There had been problems in finding high calibre students during the year and Mrs Haines had worked considerable overtime. Sadly, the situation had been compounded by the discovery that there had been some embezzlement by ticket sales staff, although the money had been recovered. The locomotives were all in working order and one carriage was still with Steamtown (this would have been for vacuum brake fitting).

The management of the railway was taken over on 1st November, 1988, by Frazer Crawley, who had joined the railway in May 1988 as assistant manager. There was not to be a new assistant manager but Mrs Betty Short, who first started at Whipsnade in February 1988, had become a member of salaried staff, working for three days a week in the ticket office and on clerical and other work. The other staff at this time were Richard Stanghan as Chief Engineer and Ian Gordon (part time), both having started in May 1987, together with Peter Haines who stayed on with the railway until he decided to retire at the end of May 1989.

The 1989 season got off to a good start and encouraged the new manager to request the renovation of two carriages, the first of which was completed in time for the August Bank Holiday traffic, which brought the useable carriage stock up to eight vehicles. After the retirement of Peter Haines, Mrs Anne Crawley joined the railway in July 1989 to assist with the station end of operations and the bookkeeping in order to allow her husband more time on the engineering side. The good start to the season fell away towards the end, however, when the zoo introduced a free road train service as an experiment at weekends and school half-term holidays. The intention of the zoo was to increase the entry charge for the following year but provide the road train as a free service to all visitors. In the end, the railway carried nearly 93,000 passengers, although this was in close proportion to the zoo visitor figures which had also fallen from the previous year. The figures had received some assistance from the re-introduction of Christmas running which was an effort to operate the railway at times other than peak season when the maximum number of visitors are in the park. In the past, the railway had operated at Christmas, but the practice had ceased around 1977/78. The experiment was successful and the railway continues to be 're-opened' whenever there are school holidays or Bank Holidays, the choice of traction between steam or diesel depending on the likely numbers in the park. Whenever possible, a steam locomotive is used at Christmas for 'Santa Specials' - the train crew usually appearing dressed in more exotic garb than normal to suit the season! In his end of year report Mr Crawley expressed his hope to steam *Chevallier* occasionally and noted that 'only minimal track widening is required to overcome her wheelbase problems, this is on my programme of improvements.' The difficulty with *Chevallier* was not her condition, Peter Haines had brought her back into working order several years before, but Mr and Mrs Haines considered the long wheelbase of the locomotive damaged the track and had withdrawn her voluntarily and she had remained languishing in the back of the shed. The issue reached a head when Sir William McAlpine, who had remained the owner of the locomotive and had not transferred her to the ownership of Pleasurerail, received an enquiry from the Welsh Highland (1964) Company whose representatives visited Whipsnade to view the locomotive. Mr McAlpine was prepared to sell the engine in order to see her returned to use, although she would have required re-gauging for use on the Welsh Highland Railway. Mr Crawley did not wish to see the locomotive leave Whipsnade and rapidly arranged to fit *Chevallier* with vacuum brakes and bring her back into service. This was accomplished in time for the 1990 season and *Chevallier* has remained in use since. It is true that *Chevallier* is a large engine but it is not felt that she damages the track sufficiently to render her unusable, although it is acknowledged that she is not comfortable over the points and curve at the end of the old station/yard. There are plans to ease this curve which may resolve the problem for *Chevallier*. *Superior* and *Excelsior* had continued to work well as had the diesels and Major Monson had asked for quotations to be obtained for overhauling *Conqueror*. The manager then looked to the future which was now felt to be rosy for the zoo, and for the railway if developed along with the zoo. A new zoo development plan looked to increase visitor numbers to around 700,000 over five years with a switch to all services being covered within the admission fee. This was a move favoured by Mr Crawley who saw this as an opportunity to invest in the railway and expand before the review of the operating agreement with the Society came up. He therefore drew up a separate report in favour of the principle towards the end of 1989. The idea was that by 1991 people would cease to bring their own cars into the park and the internal transport system would consist of the road train and the railway, either in its present form or with an extended line.

Takeover by Whipsnade

An apparently melancholy ceremony was carried out on Sunday 28th October, 1990. At 3.30 pm *Superior*, 'cleaned as never before' in the words of Frazer Crawley and sporting a laurel wreath and black headlamp, approached Whipsnade Central station. The sound of three detonators exploding saluted the last train to be run at Whipsnade under the auspices of Pleasurerail. Such a solemn event in the past would mean the closing act of a railway, fortunately in this case it signalled only the end of an era and the start of a new one. Pleasurerail had operated trains in the park for 20 years, carrying a record 113,892 passengers in its final year of independent operation. The railway had now been transferred to the Zoological Society of London. The Society had, in fact, not only purchased the railway, but Pleasurerail itself, thus a proposal first raised in 1984 had been revived and now finally taken place.

As already described, the mid to late 1980s had been worrying times financially for the park and the railway. In 1989, a spokesman had told the press that Whipsnade needed 600,000 visitors a year to break even, a figure well above the actual attendances and showing that Whipsnade had not been covering its expenses for a long time. For many years the Society had been in receipt of £2,000,000 deficit revenue funding from the government, although there was no statutory obligation for this support, and in 1987 Ministers requested a study, this being undertaken by Peat Marwick McLintock. As early as July 1987 Major Monson had written to the Society expressing concern about the lack of animals beside the line which resulted in complaints from passengers, the uncertainty about the future of Whipsnade and asking that Pleasurerail be allowed some involvement in the preparation of the Peat Marwick McLintock report. Some discussions must have been going on behind the scenes because on 21st November, 1988, David Jones wrote a lengthy letter to Major Monson confirming that Whipsnade had a considerable operating deficit and the Society were seeking a capital investment from a partner in the leisure field with whom the ZSL would naturally discuss the transport situation in the park before coming back to Pleasurerail with a definite proposal, the interesting sentence was 'given all of this we are not in fact moving away from the principle of taking over the railway as we discussed with you previously....'

Supporters of Whipsnade had, over the years, held the view that Whipsnade was considered the poor relation of Regents Park and anticipated the worst. What actually happened was the opposite. The report published by Peat Marwick McLintock summarised that the zoo's were tourist attractions and should be run at arms length from the Society itself. This resulted in the formation of a company called Zoo Operations Ltd (wholly owned by ZSL) which was formed to turn things around. Far from selling Whipsnade off as some had feared, it was seen that with large amounts of available land and a strong background of innovation in the keeping of animals (Whipsnade had started well before Safari Parks came on the scene) the real answer was to give the park a facelift and with new management and strong marketing make Whipsnade the way into the future. The zoo had already changed its name to 'Whipsnade Wild Animal Park' in 1988 and work on the new image proceeded apace. Although the Society had proposed a prospectus and identified a possible partner for the lease of the core business at Whipsnade, the deal fell through, primarily because a suitable 'first refusal' could not be agreed in the event of a subsequent sale. The Society Council was, and remains, conscious of their heritage and felt it inappropriate to have no control over a potential partner, the deal being formally cancelled on 1st August, 1989.

In the meantime communications with Pleasurerail seem to have lapsed somewhat, for on 13th October, 1989, Major Monson wrote to Mr Jones pointing out that a year ago he had asked for information about the Society's plans for Whipsnade and had been told that negotiations were in hand. Major Monson had been patiently waiting for news, but had now been told by Frazer Crawley that he had heard a number of important decisions had been made about the park. In reply, the Society confirmed that the idea of taking a partner had been dropped and instead they were looking for alternative sources of finance in order to retain control of the park. The letter confirmed that the idea of banning cars from inside the park had been abandoned, and that investment in the internal transport system would have to be an intregal part of the re-development programme, but at the present time ZSL did not want to make any definite proposals until they knew the necessary finance was available. The Society were however doing their homework and had realised that the original operating agreement, which had come into effect on 1st January, 1973, ran for a period of 20 years and, it may be recalled had a clause to the effect that not later than two years before the expiry of the agreement the parties should consult as to the future arrangements. An internal zoo memo written on 5th December, 1989, asked 'Has anybody made an official approach to Pleasurerail to take over the Railway?' The answer to the question, written by hand on the original memo was 'Yes', the writer had asked Sir William to donate the railway - and his reply had been 'No' This reply is not too surprising considering the investment put in, and with the other shareholders in Pleasurerail to consider! In fact, Sir Gordon Booth, a former diplomat and then senior advisor to Hanson PLC, had been detailed by the ZSL Council to agree the principal terms of a sale. This was achieved, Peter Denton, clerk to the ZSL Council proceeded to work up the details.

The 1989/90 season had been the best ever for the railway, carrying 113,892 passengers and by March 1990 discussions were under way between Pleasurerail and ZSL. On 6th June, 1990, the Society were provided with the Pleasurerail accounts for the year ended 31st October, 1989. While these showed an operating loss, by deducting various sums which would cease under new owners, the operation would show a profit of £27,783. A valuation had been prepared by Mr Hinchcliffe and Pleasurerail were prepared to sell the railway and issued share capital of the company for £350,000 (profits for the current season to be retained by the current shareholders.) Further meetings took place, the Society being confident that the business would be profitable under their ownership, and a ZSL Project Appraisal gave the reasons for a purchase as being: increased income, the removal of an anomaly (the railway being the only concessionaire left in the park), an improved marketing stance (a reference to the ambition of introducing an all inclusive admission charge), the opportunity for an 'all in' ticket to allow a price increase while conveying an impression of added value to visitors, and the opportunity to develop additional income from sponsorship and business functions. By August a counter offer of £170,000 had been made, subject to certain understandings and conditions including there being a minimum £50,000 cash in the company. The Pleasurerail reply turned this offer down, but gave a revised figure which would be acceptable, and by September the negotiations had been concluded. The figure agreed was £200,000 which was to include £50,000 cash assets, the remainder representing the equipment, but not including *Chevallier* which was Sir William McAlpine's personal property. The agreement included the retention of the manager and staff, which numbered five as previously detailed. In the event, the official 'last train' under Pleasurerail was slightly premature. The takeover which was due on 31st October, 1990, did not actually occur until 5th November, 1990, on which date Pleasurerail Ltd duly ceased trading and subsequently, by special resolution, the company name was changed to Whipsnade Wild Animal Park Ltd, this taking effect on 12th December, 1990, and actually registered on 10th January, 1991. The actual signing ceremony was undertaken on 5th November, 1990 with the Pleasurerail Board being present and Peter Denton representing ZSL, in the offices of Winters, the chartered accountants in Holburn. As a result, Peter Denton achieved at a stroke an ambition which he never thought would come to fruition - he was a Director of a railway company!

The results of the new management arrangements for the park continued to bear fruit with progressively rising numbers of visitors. Zoo Operations Ltd no longer exists having ceased to trade in October 1992, the railway is now run as a division (or department) of Whipsnade Wild Animal Park, the trading company for which is Whipsnade Wild Animal Park Ltd. The number of visitors in 1992/93 was 425,830 and the railway carried 29 per cent of these, 123,629 in all, both figures actually representing a fall from the highs of a couple of years before. The park now operates on a budget set each year for a specified number of visitors and the effect of the changes which have been made are illustrated by the 1994 'break even' budget which was set at 375,000 visitors compared with the 600,000 stated to be required five years earlier, additions above the budget figure obviously representing profit. The present situation is that while both Whipsnade and Regents Park are divisions of the Zoological Society of London, they are financially independent of each other. While problems in recent times have continued surrounding Regents Park and may have affected the reputation of the Society as a whole, it is not felt that there has been any major impact on Whipsnade.

The railway was handed over complete and in generally good order and the general manager, Mr Crawley, remained in that post under the new ownership. Three of the four steam locomotives, together with the two Fowler diesels, were in working order (although only *Hector* was equipped with vacuum brakes). Only *Conqueror* was out of service and in need of extensive work. At the time, it was planned that the restoration would be done on site by the railway's own staff and it was intended that the engine would be back in service for the railway's silver jubilee in August 1995, although the need for additional outside help was foreseen if the intensified traffic operations envisaged by the new owners took place as planned. To have *Conqueror* overhauled by outside contractors had been investigated and the quotations ranged from £50,000 to £100,000. Of the other rolling stock, there were eight carriages available for use. Five were equipped with vacuum brakes and of the 28 seat capacity type, two were piped only with hand brakes and also of 28 seat capacity, and a further vehicle was listed as having a hand brake only and capacity of 22 seats. In addition, there was an open carriage undergoing complete restoration and conversion to 40 seat capacity, and a further coach awaiting restoration which would be of a 32 seat capacity, or 28 seats plus 4 wheelchairs. The track was reported to be in generally good order although some remedial work was required in places. The staff at this time consisted of the General Manager who was responsible for all aspects of running the railway, two assistant manageresses who were based at the station to run the platforms and handle most dealings with the public, a Chief Engineer responsible for footplate tuition as well as the stock, plant and track and deputising for the mechanical side of the operation in the absence of the General Manager, and an Engineer/chief driver to assist the Chief Engineer with tuition and deputise in his absence. In addition, there were brief job definitions for staff at the station, drivers and fireman, all of which were part time posts.

There were clearly very high hopes for the railway under its new ownership and a report was prepared by the General Manager giving details and costings for several future developments. The intention was clearly to define the present position of the railway and offer thoughts for the new owners to help them decide the direction they wanted to take with the line, and the degree to which they may wish to invest in it. The report stated that from 1st March, 1991, the railway would be expected to carry 100 per cent of visitors to the park. Since the figure for the previous year was 25 per cent of visitors this would represent a huge jump. The explanation lays in the plan for park visitors to pay an admission price inclusive of both entrance to the zoo and a trip on the railway, a proposal which had of course been raised before but never implemented. Implicit in such a policy was, of course, investment in additional locomotives, stock and infrastructure.

Although there had been many plans previously covering zoo developments and expansion of the railway which had failed to come to implementation, there was some justification this time. The dolphinarium near Whipsnade Central used to have an additional charge but this had been dropped some years before. The zoo now had free bird of prey flying displays and there were free talks, then by keepers and now provided by the zoo education department. The road train service had also become free in the autumn of 1989 and since the trend in entertainment parks was also leading towards a policy of an all-inclusive admission price the proposal was once again raised in relation to the railway.

The other issue at this time was the possibility of constructing a substantial extension to the length of the track into the rest of the park, either in conjunction with the 'Trail Breaker' (the road train which transports visitors around the roads in other parts of the park) or even as the sole transport system in the park. The report gives no references to additional track construction, only a brief mention at the end to the future possibility of the railway becoming more than just a ride, but part of the park's transport infrastructure.

The report estimated that it would cost £25,000 to construct five more carriages (three with vacuum brakes, two piped only, all of 40 seats) which would provide a third train to add to the two already available or, at least, nearly so. It was also estimated that at a cost of £2,500 each the existing carriages could be altered to the 40 seat pattern. The railway was limited to five-coach trains due to the length of the existing platform at Whipsnade Central, plus the additional factor that *Excelsior* would not be able to cope with a six-coach train although this would not be a problem for *Superior* or *Chevallier* or, indeed, *Conqueror* if it were returned to service.

The other option was, of course, to run a four-train service at peak times. The use of two-way radios had been successfully introduced in 1990 and had worked well for two-train operation. To handle passengers with a four-train service it would be necessary to use both platforms at Whipsnade Central and adopt section signalling to satisfy the Railway Inspectorate. If this had been adopted then a number of changes would have been required to the methods of working the railway, including the adoption of seven track sections rather than the existing six, although the seventh section was actually the south side of the loop in Whipsnade Central. Attached to the report was a drawing showing the revised section locations on the circuit and it is intriguing to note that although the new section was proposed to be simply the south loop line, the other section locations vary from the present positions.

The question of handling so many extra passengers was also considered. The issuing of tickets from the booking office would be eliminated by an inclusive park admission fee, and by constructing 'holding pens' combined with new exit gates at the far end of the platform, complete train loads of people could have their tickets checked and be ready for boarding as soon as a train arrived. An experiment along these lines had been carried out over the 1990 August Bank Holiday weekend and the reduction in loading and unloading times had been dramatic. A proposed plan of the arrangements was included in the report, although it has never been implemented.

Aside from raising the possibility of introducing concrete sleepers over sections of 30 ft at a time in order progressively to reduce maintenance, nothing else was planned concerning the circuit itself. The yard area, however, was detailed as requiring lifting and re-laying, with the opportunity to be taken of revising the layout from what was described as the 'awkward present arrangement.' The significant changes described and detailed on a drawing would have involved the construction of a four-road carriage shed alongside the engine shed; a new Mess Room/Workshop/Store behind the engine shed; a fuel store in the corner between the veterinary hospital, old children's zoo and road; and a turntable more or less beside Whipsnade Junction signal box. The railway owned the parts for this turntable and the intention was to even up the wear caused by the circular nature of the track circuit on wheel flanges, tyres, bearings and couplings by occasionally turning the carriages. Several areas around the yard were intended to be concreted over and it was envisaged that after all this work the area would be suitable for opening to the public. In addition to the capital costs of all this work the manager pointed out that increasingly intense services would require more expenditure on maintenance.

An interesting section at the end of the report offers some thoughts on the possibilities which could be the subject of future developments. These included the enticing prospect of constructing a luxury train offering visitors the prospect of eating an evening meal while sedately travelling through Asia and Africa. Another idea was the construction of a small museum in the yard combined with an 'Engine Encounter' guided tour, a progression perhaps of the display some years before of the Zambezi railway stock and part of the reason for bringing *Nutty* to the railway (*see later*). The overall concept was very much based on the perception that public interest in purely animal attractions was fading and the intention was to provide complementary attractions which would reinstate Whipsnade as a leader in its field, as it had been on opening in 1931.

Many of the schemes which were envisaged became the subject of considerable further work and discussion through 1991 and the following year. The schemes for extending the railway were sufficiently developed that Frazer Crawley and Chris Webster, the park operations manager, went to Poland to check on available equipment and it was planned that tenders would be made for track and concrete sleepers which were to become available from Broughton

Moor (*see later*). At one point, the proposal appeared to have been approved by the Zoological Society, but shortly afterwards was cancelled on financial grounds. More complete details of the extension schemes are given later (Plans that Never Happened) together with the 'Wine and Dine' train scheme.

In the event, not only did the expansion plans fail to reach fruition, but the first season of operation under the ownership of the zoo did not go well financially. The fare for the 1990 season was £1.50 for adults and 80p for children, however during the 'Steam Weekend' the fares had been slashed by 50 per cent with the result that the railway carried 52 per cent of the visitors on those days. In August there had been a further experiment which offered an optional 'all in' admission price to the park which had resulted in an increase in visitors riding on the railway from 23 per cent to 60 per cent. Encouraged by these results, and in line with the zoo policy of phasing out additional charges and covering everything in the price of admission, the zoo decided that for the 1991 season the admission price to the park would be increased by £1; of this, 50p was considered an actual price rise and the other 50p represented the fare on the railway. The result was a large increase in passengers, and a substantial operating loss for the railway. At the time of the zoo's purchase the accounting period changed. This does not affect peak season figures, but does alter the allocation of end of season passenger loadings. Allowing for this, the 1990 total of 113,892 passengers (25 per cent of park visitors) jumped to 173,815 (35.8 per cent of visitors) in 1991. In 1990, the operating profit had been some £40,000, but this became a loss of about £23,000 in 1991. For the sake of completeness, in order to even out the distortions resulting from the change of accounting periods, the following year produced 167,779 passengers (39 per cent of visitors) and financially the railway just about broke even. By 1993, the fares experiment was ended and the railway returned to profit, the 1993 passenger figures being 123,629, representing 29 per cent of visitors. It is worth noting that the 1993 figures were better than any year under Pleasurerail and were only exceeded by the two years of the experimental fare structure.

There was also a second reason for the reported loss in 1991. It is of interest to note that although the track is a circle, Pleasurerail, which had been formed to build and operate railways and as a transport company was, for VAT purposes, zero rated, and had operated the line as a transport system. This was achieved by transporting people to a point and then transporting them back again. It just so happened that trains performed the return journey over a different route from that used to go outwards! It was understood that this was assisted by the existence of Umfolozi Halt, which was still in good condition in 1991 and remained so into 1992, although subsequently many of the sleepers were removed, resulting in the present ruinous state. When the railway was purchased by the Society, the prudent decision was made by the management to account for the VAT until the status of the railway as part of the overall operation was clarified. This resulted in payments of some £20,000 per year with an obvious effect on profits. Mr Crawley proposed the construction of a new station or halt near the farm crossing, just short of the animal paddocks, which could have been used by passengers wishing to join or alight, on the basis that any ambiguity concerning Umfolozi Halt where, of course, it was no longer feasible for passengers to actually use it as a station, would be removed. In fact, the financial controller of the park clarified the position, in that there was a precedent, set by another park railway elsewhere in the country, to support the premise that the railway should be treated as a transport system. This was accepted by the Customs & Excise, with the result that all VAT paid for the previous 18 months was refunded. Unfortunately, the status of the railway, in common with other park oriented systems, was changed in the November 1994 Budget, resulting in the park having to pay VAT on the railway revenue from the start of the 1995 season. This will reduce the revenue of the park to the tune of £15,000 per annum, an amount that would otherwise be invested into the future of the railway.

Equus Ferreus Semper Vincit
(The Iron Horse Always Conquers)

The roots of the railway lay in the Bowater's Industrial Railway in Kent, a connection continued by the use of steam locomotives and stock from that line throughout the first twenty years of its life under the auspices of Pleasurerail. The railway motto and coat of arms had been in use from the opening of the railway, an elegant crest having been displayed on the locomotives and carriages, although latterly this has fallen out of use. It seems appropriate to mention it at this point, since the next few years were to see something which was new to the railway - the exchange of locomotives for short periods with one of the other two remaining 2 ft 6 in. gauge railways in Britain. There had been earlier connections with the Welshpool & Llanfair line in Wales, which included the acquisition of a Fowler diesel locomotive, but the 1990s and the revised management arrangements saw the beginning of noticeably closer links with this railway.

Frazer Crawley, the Whipsnade railway manager, was also a member of the Welshpool & Llanfair Railway and on 12th September, 1990, had written to the Narrow Gauge Railway Museum Trust offering a home for *Nutty*. This fascinating little locomotive was built by Sentinel Ltd at Shrewsbury in 1929. It had a small, vertical, high pressure water tube boiler, two horizontal cylinders, and drive was transmitted by a chain from the engine crankshaft to the back axle on the left hand side. On the other side, the two axles were coupled by a second chain. The locomotive had been found by Welshpool & Llanfair members at the premises of the London Brick Company near Peterborough where it was the last of a fleet of Sentinels which had worked on the mile long line of 2 ft 11 in. gauge, moving wagon loads of bricks from the presses to the kilns. The name *Nutty* arose from the nickname of Mr John Rowell who was a charge hand fitter at the brickworks and who worked there for 48 years. The locomotive arrived at the W&L on 28th June, 1964, was re-gauged and overhauled, making its test run in February 1965, after which the cab, bonnet and chain cases were fitted. *Nutty* became the W&L railway's No. 5 and worked maintenance trains and, although not approved for the work, was also used on occasion to work passenger trains on a short shuttle service during emergencies. After 1966, the loco was rarely used and on 23rd October, 1971, it was sent to the Narrow Gauge Museum Trust at Towyn, Merioneth.

The offer by Mr Crawley was accepted and *Nutty* went to Whipsnade, the delivery note being dated 27th February, 1991. There were high hopes of restoring it again to full working order later in the year. The locomotive went to Whipsnade on a lease made between the Trustees and Zoo Operations Ltd and there was some delay in signing the paperwork, since it does not appear to have been finally completed until about September 1992. The actual terms were for a 20 year period running from 1st November, 1991 with a peppercorn rent and the normal conditions one would expect in such an agreement. On arrival, the locomotive was still in complete condition, subsequently it was dismantled for refurbishing and, in August 1993, Mr Crawley replied to the Museum Trust's annual check that the frames were ready to lift from the axles and the boiler was at Maskells in Bedford. Progress had been slow, since this was an enthusiasts' project and time was limited. Sadly, the hopes of restoration have not been fulfilled and the engine has remained in pieces in the Whipsnade yard. The frames and wheels are in the yard on the rails and are capable of being moved but most of the remaining parts are stacked on a wagon in the yard beside the engine shed. The boiler remains at the workshop in Bedford. Indeed, the Trustees' representative was concerned to find that it was being stored in the open and not under cover or protected when he visited Maskells in August 1994. Mr Crawley left the railway in February 1994 and the present management feel that Whipsnade does not have the resources to undertake the necessary restoration work. The future of the engine is now under discussion again with its owners. Whilst of great historic interest, and it must be hoped that this little locomotive will be fully restored again, it has to be said that it would hardly have been suitable for actually working at Whipsnade. The engine was built for single person operation and the crew would be forgiven for having some anxiety in sharing the very cramped cab with a boiler working at some 230 psi in the midst of a paddock of wild animals!

There was another Royal visitor to the park in 1991 when Prince Edward officially opened the new 'Tiger Falls' attraction on 23rd May. This time, there was to be no train ride, even though the new exhibit is just behind Whipsnade Central. The arrangements, however, did require that a carefully timed train should arrive just as the Royal party approached the level crossing at Central Avenue from the 'Cafe on the Lake', so that they would have to 'wait' for the train to pass - some recompense, if inadvertent, for the train being kept waiting by Prince Philip ten years before? Ian Gordon and Anne Crawley were on the footplate of *Superior* which was to handle the train, the passengers on which were zoo pensioners and guests. In order to achieve the perfect timing required, the locomotive crew were in constant radio contact with Central station, so that they could be told to 'slow down' or 'speed up' as they progressed on the circuit. Unfortunately, it became apparent that the Royal party were in danger of beating the train and the instructions to 'speed up' became increasingly urgent. The train managed to make it in time but, in the process, it is reckoned that the fastest circuit ever recorded was set on that trip - it is said that many of the pensioners were shaking as they alighted from the train!

The Welshpool connection arose again with, as the W&L Society Journal described it '.... a rare opportunity of seeing unfamiliar and interesting motive power on our line.' On 28th August, 1991, the Whipsnade locomotive *Chevallier* arrived at the Welsh line for a loan period. Unfortunately, things did not get off to a good start, a trip up the unfamiliar railway revealed problems with *Chevallier's* axle boxes. The Welshpool people immediately raised the engine to start correcting the problem. When the Whipsnade team, which consisted of Frazer Crawley, his wife Anne and Ian Gordon, arrived in their Land Rover they found their engine up on blocks in a siding under floodlights with the axle boxes removed and being re-metalled! The problem was caused by blocked oilways and wicks which were too small. On the short circuit at 'home' this weakness had not come to light, but the longer and somewhat tougher nature of the W&L quickly showed up the fault. By 31st August, 1991, *Chevallier* was back in working order and handled a freight train to Cyfronedd, followed by double-heading an evening passenger train with *The Countess* to Welshpool. On the Sunday morning, *Chevallier* took charge of its first train to Welshpool and back before double heading the 6.30 pm train from Llanfair. Some amusement over the weekend was achieved when the Whipsnade party's Land Rover was loaded onto a W&L bogie wagon and shunted up and down the line, including on a two-vehicle train hauled by *Dougal*, a diminutive 0-4-0 locomotive built in 1946 for use at the Provan Works of Glasgow Corporation Gas Department by Andrew Barclay, Sons & Co. Ltd, of Kilmarnock. The locomotive is works number 2207 and remained at Provan until 1958. Following changes of ownership and an overhaul it arrived at Welshpool in 1969. *Chevallier* remained at the W&L until January 1992 and, although its use was restricted since it was not fitted with continuous brakes, it helped out with 'Santa Specials' before returning to Whipsnade.

The May Bank Holiday earlier in 1991 had also seen the first of what has become an annual event at Whipsnade - the 'Steam Up' weekend. The event derives from a Father's Day event at Whipsnade and has become a steam gala at the zoo with visiting traction engines, steam rollers, showmen's engines, steam powered lorries and large scale model traction engines. These visiting engines park in the area around Central Avenue or in the car park behind the station and drive round the circuit of roads with the railway in the centre. Naturally, the railway contributes to the event with special workings, and 'Steam Up' has turned the May Bank Holiday into the busiest weekend of the year. For the 1992 event, *Superior* and *Chevallier* worked the passenger trains while *Excelsior* was also in steam. In addition, for the first time, Whipsnade received a visiting locomotive for the weekend. This was the small Andrew Barclay, Sons & Co. locomotive, *Dougal*, from the Welshpool & Llanfair Railway. This locomotive is not a 'traffic' engine and at Whipsnade acted as a working display for members of the public in and around the Whipsnade Central station loop line. The opportunity was taken, however, to drive *Dougal* around the complete circuit at least once as a light engine. A record number of passengers carried in one day on the railway was set during this event - 4,099. The last train of the day was also a special working. With *Superior* as train engine and *Excelsior* as pilot, the most unusual sight was provided at

Chevallier heads a train through the old Rhino paddock which now houses other animals, in this case passing a group of Pere David's deer.   *Author*

Superior on the level crossing enters Whipsnade Central on Christmas Eve 1994. The frost was so heavy the park had the appearance of a light covering of snow.   *Author*

Superior in Round Close paddock. This view was taken in 1994 from the top of the Helter Skelter which at that time was located near the level crossing - in 1995 it was moved into the playground/fairground area on the other side of the station.   *Author*

The 'Junior Friends of Whipsnade' visit on 29th April, 1995, included painting the carriages!
Carrie Thomas

Superior and *Chevallier* at Whipsnade Central before the start of the day's work during the May 1995 'Steam Up' weekend. Passenger trains only work from the north (far side) platform, *Superior* is on the south road to pick up the set of coaches left in the platform overnight and will shunt across into the other platform when *Chevallier* has departed with the first train.   *Author*

Chevallier has just cleared the loop turnout and is about to cross Central Avenue and enter Whipsnade Central in May 1995.   *Author*

Chevallier in Valley Meadow / Cut Throat paddock passes a nilgai in the foreground, on the slope behind the train are onager.   *Author*

Chevallier has just passed Umfolozi Halt (marked by the flagpole) and rounded the curve just after the platform, Yak are just visible behind the train.   *Author*

The railway shop in its present form. Passengers pass through the opening between the fence and shop wall in the centre of the picture and purchase tickets from a window which faces the tracks.   *Author*

The view back into the original station. The turnout in the foreground originally led the track into the south road of the station. When the circuit was completed the main line, which arrives from the left of the picture, was joined up at this point. The slightly raised platform is still intact in this 1994 view, as is the north platform line and the siding beside the old childrens zoo boundary which has subsequently been lifted. The Soham signal box is being stored on the platform.   *Author*

The Welshpool & Llanfair locomotive No. 14 (SLR 85) pilots *Superior* over Central Avenue and into Central station during the May 1993 'Steam Up'.   *Peter Denton*

Excelsior with the goods train and *Chevallier* with a service passenger train at Whipsnade Central during the May 1993 'Steam Up'.   *Mike Wade*

As a train departs under the footbridge a clear view is possible of the Whipsnade Central station layout. The Union flag and balloons are combined 'VE' Day and May 'Steam Up' decorations.

Author

The level crossing, signal box (moved from the original station site in 1973) and Whipsnade Central station. In the trees behind the box is the 'Tiger Falls' enclosure, previously this was 'Wolf Wood'.

Author

Whipsnade Junction signal box pictured in 1994. The main line is in the foreground, the line into the yard can be seen in the centre of this view. *Author*

Early morning in April 1995, *left to right* are: a Bowaters wagon frame in the early stages of conversion into a coach, *Victor*, *Superior* being prepared for service and repairs in progress to the panels of a coach. The scaffolding has been erected around the shed in preparation for the new cladding, and the temporary screen to hide the work from the birds of prey is visible to the left of *Victor*. *Author*

Whipsnade of a double headed steam train traversing the circuit, a sight probably not previously seen since the very early years, and almost certainly not since 1974.

The next Whipsnade engine to be given a 'holiday' in Wales was *Superior* which arrived at Llanfair on 1st September, 1992 for the Welshpool line's steam gala. Within about an hour of arriving *Superior* was in steam, after which she was prepared for the following weekend. This time there were no embarrassments and *Superior* ran successfully, assisting *The Countess* with one of the two passenger train sets operated during the gala weekend. The engine continued to be used on an occasional basis, finally helping out with a special train on the last day of the operating season, following which she left for Whipsnade, arriving home on 5th October, 1992.

The series of exchanges continued the following year with the loan of the W&L locomotive No. 14 (also known as SLR 85) to Whipsnade for the 1993 May 'steam up' weekend. The locomotive went to Whipsnade in late April and returned immediately after the gala weekend. This locomotive is a 2-6-2 tank built by the Hunslet Engine Co. Ltd of Leeds in 1954. It was the last of 32 similar locomotives supplied to the Sierra Leone Railway and had been shipped back to Britain in 1975. Although the engine was working through paddocks housing Asian animals rather than African, the cowcatcher fitted to the front of the engine certainly looked the part! Most of the workings with this engine were double headers with SLR 85 as pilot and *Superior* as train engine, a situation to some extent enforced by the adapted coupling arrangements required. The second service train over the weekend was worked by *Chevallier* and, as another innovation, *Excelsior* worked a 'goods' train consisting of all nine Broughton Moor wagons, including the delivery of coal for the exhibiting steam road engines. If the effect for visitors of the double-headed service trains was fairly spectacular, even more impressive was the special train for the exhibitors at the 'steam up' which ran after the normal park closing time on the Sunday night. This was also a double-headed train, but hauling nine carriages and ran round three circuits, two of which were non-stop.

The series of locomotive exchanges had been largely inspired by Mr Crawley. When he left the railway in early 1994 the line only had one remaining full-time employee and no exchange took place for the 1994 'steam up'. However, the railway maintained the tradition of novel workings, this time with a diesel-hauled 'demonstration' freight train working around the circuit in addition to the two steam-hauled passenger trains, *Excelsior* being out of action while being re-tubed.

Despite the improving figures and clear evidence of turning round the fortunes of the park, there has not been the kind of money available for the substantial investments in stock and infrastructure initially hoped for.

This point is reinforced when looking at the report prepared by Major P.M. Olver, Assistant Chief Inspecting Officer of Railways on 19th January, 1991, following an inspection of the line, and considers the subsequent work carried out. The inspection of Whipsnade Central station had included a lengthy discussion between the inspector and Mr Crawley concerning the problems likely to arise from catering for longer and more frequent trains. It was envisaged that within two years there would be a need for eight coach trains. The platform, which can accommodate five coaches would, as a consequence, need to be lengthened and Major Olver did not foresee any difficulty in moving the turnout at the east end of the station further up the slope near to the pedestrian overbridge and reconstructing the east end of the passenger platform. In the event, train lengths have not increased and such work has not been necessary. The road crossing at the top of the climb from Central station was described as having a full barrier of early Godwin Warren origin, together with single sets of steady amber and twin red flashing road signals on each approach. The approach from the south carried works traffic, the other approach with the barrier being for the one-way traffic of park visitors. Major Olver felt the crossing badly needed renovation and to be put into good working order before the next summer season. In the event, however, the one-way system in the park was changed a couple of years after the inspection and the barrier arm removed completely! The report proceeded with reference to the inspector having 'complained most bitterly that the coaches were not fitted with vacuum brakes' on his last visit. He had agreed that the first aim was that a proportion of the coaches should be fitted and the remainder equipped with through pipes. The railway was able to show that this had been achieved and Major Olver was 'very heartened' to hear that the 1992 budget included a considerable sum to convert the remaining piped coaches to fully vacuum braked and for new construction to be fully equipped. The Major 'considered this to be an excellent position and a great increase in the safety of the running of the railway.' At the end of 1994, however, there are still several piped only coaches, these being marshalled between the locomotive and the fully braked vehicles in trains.

The improvements made in the zoo to enhance the appeal to visitors had included constructing a loose surface road through Cut Throat paddock and Valley Meadow which visitors could opt to join in a one way direction by turning right off Cut Throat Avenue at the end of the Dagnall paddock and taking their own cars through the 'Animals of Asia' in a safari park style drive. The road offers a different route through the paddocks and cuts back to rejoin the main zoo road by the car park opposite the Woodfield paddock. As a result, there is a right angle level crossing with the railway in the old rhino paddock. Major Olver inspected the crossing and found it to have been 'put in in substantial fashion with cross-members of 75 lb. rail on which the running rails are welded to gauge and then mass concrete poured both in the 2 ft 6 in. gauge and also on either cess.' Unfortunately, he went on to say he was 'alarmed' to see that there was no checkrail or angle put in to keep the railway flangeways clear and predicted the railway would have trouble with the concrete breaking up. Further discussion then took place concerning signalling at the crossing, expressing the opinion that there should be white flashing lights to show that the barriers are down and the road traffic signals are working. The railway was clearly thinking along these lines and by May 1991, detailed drawings had been prepared for a comprehensive installation which would have included amber, then flashing red, road signals, flashing white lights for railway drivers and an audible warning device. In the event, no system at all has been installed, road and rail drivers being warned of the crossing by signs only. There have been no problems at the crossing, which is perhaps not surprising, since not only are trains only travelling at about 8 mph, but car drivers also are moving very slowly. The only obvious problem which could arise is in the event of a car driver being so intent on watching the animals, usually yak and camels at this point, that they fail to look where they are going, but assuming drivers will be intent on avoiding running down animals it seems unlikely they will overlook the presence of a railway!

The 1986 inspections of the railway had included some biting criticism of the track. Much progress had been made in the intervening years, for the only comment this time concerned a shortage of ballast for a considerable length of the main line and a lack of ballast shoulders to hold the track in place laterally. The inspector felt this should be included in a programme for maintenance even though it could not be put right immediately, observing that if the work were not carried out it would lead to accelerated deterioration of the sleepers and a rise in the cost of maintenance for the railway. The remainder of the report deals with the tunnel and the inspector's concern that it was shared by the railway with animals. This area had been the source of problems as far back as the completion of the circuit. These had been resolved by the construction of the new ha-ha at the Cut Throat end, although animals had always been able to traverse the tunnel from the Round Close end, but not pass into Cut Throat paddock. When the ha-ha was built, the fence on the 'inside' of the tracks extended from the tunnel parallel to the track for some distance into the paddock. The fence alignment at the time of this inspection must have been different from that which is in place today, and certainly different from the original arrangement, since animals were now able to circumvent the ha-ha, in fact the zoo had started to fill in the ha-ha ditch. The main problem identified was that as a result the railway track through the tunnel was becoming covered with mud and dirt and was 'totally unsuitable for trains to run through it in its present state'. In the view of Major Olver, the track should be taken up and relaid with concrete up to the railhead surface. The effect would be like a length of tramway forming a shared walk for animals and a railway. There were evidently further discussions and a measure of compromise reached, with the inspector being prepared to accept the creation of 'ballasted or proper paths' down to the railway track on each approach to the tunnel, together with the track being dug out and completely reballasted or concreted on each approach before the start of the next summer season.

Despite the compromise, however, it is clear that Major Olver remained troubled by the whole idea of animals and railway sharing the tunnel and urged that further thought be applied to the situation. While accepting that train speeds were low and most of the animals fairly small and unlikely to cause a derailment, he forcefully made the point that from a moral angle the effect on passengers, especially children, of an accident which killed or maimed an animal in the tunnel made the situation most undesirable. Various methods were tried to resolve the difficulty including mounting electrified 'wands' which were pushed away by passing locomotives. Unfortunately, these were regularly broken and the idea was given up after a passenger received a shock from one which caught her foot through the gap between the carriage floor and the lower edge of the side panels. Eventually it was agreed with the park management that the fences should be reinstated and the ha-ha reverted to the purpose of stopping animals from moving between the two paddocks, about 80 tons of chalk having to be dug back out of the ha-ha ditch. Even now, animals can enter the tunnel from the Round Close paddock and get as far as the embankment beside the railway at the entry end, although the ha-ha prevents them from moving completely into Cut Throat paddock. This concession is intended as an escape route for animals caught in the tunnel as a train approaches. Locomotive drivers still have to take great care on entering the tunnel since clearances are very tight and the situation can become particularly awkward in wet weather since, without a sufficient run at the slope, a train can easily slip to a standstill in this section. The ha-ha ditch at this point has always contained a considerable amount of water. As an aside, railway staff still recall with great amusement the occasion one winter when Ian Gordon was working on the track joints on the ha-ha bridge with a large spanner which slipped off the nut. Mr Gordon lost his balance as a result and fell backwards into the ice covered water. Although wet and cold, but perfectly safe, the rest of the track gang would not let him get out until he had recovered the spanner from the bottom of the freezing pool!

A further visit to the railway on 23rd August, 1991, was undertaken by Major Peter Olver of the Railway Inspectorate. It was agreed that the new open crossing protection system in the old rhino paddock where the railway was crossed by the road in the 'drive through' area was working satisfactorily and it was not necessary to install the complex automatic system which had originally been proposed. As a result of this visit, Tom Craig was asked to prepare a report on the other crossing, at the top of the climb out of the station. The report was prepared on 9th September, 1991, and concluded that the equipment was approaching the end of its useful life. This crossing had not been the scene of any serious incidents, although in about 1974 as *Conqueror* approached the junction the engine crew saw a woman drive her car onto the crossing. *Conqueror* stopped without difficulty, but despite their shouted warnings, the car driver moved neither forwards nor back with the result that the arm bounced up and down about five times on the roof of the car - apparently trying to chop the car in half. In July 1987 the barrier arm had come down on the roof of a car again, which led to an interesting discussion as to whether the car had damaged the barrier or vice versa! The report went into some detail and recommended the installation of a similar open crossing system as had worked successfully in the 'deer park'. In the event, this is roughly what happened since the barrier arm was removed when the internal one-way system was reversed, although the audible warning remains. At least there is no danger of the barrier coming into conflict with cars again!

The beginning of the 1990s saw many proposals for development within the zoo. One of the more extensive was the idea of opening up a new main entrance to the Park. A new access road would have been built from Whipsnade village and would have entered the park at the bottom of the hill near the farm crossing. The railway would have passed over the road on a bridge and the entrance itself would have been on the area occupied by the farm. The elephants would have been moved into the end of the rhino paddock and a new 'International Pavilion' station built for the railway. Mr Crawley found that a complete signal box located at Soham Mere, at the village of Soham near Cambridge, had become available for £250 and agreement was secured to purchase it for the new station. Soham station had hit the news headlines when it was subjected to a massive explosion at 1.43 am on 2nd June, 1944. A wagon in an ammunition train had caught fire and the driver and fireman detached the blazing van and tried to run forward to get it clear of the town. As the engine and wagon approached the signal box the wagon blew up. Two people were killed in the explosion and five seriously injured, the station buildings were largely destroyed and the nearby town suffered from the blast.

The original cost had seemed very reasonable but with the addition of transport, including the discovery at the last moment that it was just over the width limit which made it a 'wide load', and the hire of a suitable crane, the total expenditure turned out to be nearer £1,800. The whole project seemed to be fated. An initial attempt to collect the box with a four-wheel trailer had to be abandoned when, on turning into the car park, one of the trailer wheels detached and continued on its way - as a result of this episode the box unofficially acquired the new name of 'Three Wheel signal box'! The box is 24 ft long, 15 ft 1 in. wide, 12 ft 6 in. high and weighs 4 tons and was eventually transported to Whipsnade on 5th May, 1992; there is a video record of the removal from the site which was made for Anglia TV. Both the exterior and interior were in basically sound condition but the project which led to the purchase was eventually dropped and the railway now owned a signal box with no immediate use in mind. It remained stored on the old station platform, until receipt of a suitable offer in April 1995, it was removed by its new owner in the following month.

Over a period of time, the salaried staff of the railway had risen to five people, but 1991/92 brought another drive for economies by the zoo and three staff were made redundant. Mrs Anne Crawley (full-time) and Mrs Betty Short (part-time) had been assistant managers under Pleasurerail, being re-titled 'railway co-ordinators' after the zoo took over. Anne Crawley had reached the status of passed fireman and had also repainted *Victor* at the end of the 1992 season as well as doing construction work on one of the carriages. In the winter both ladies helped out in the shed, repainted carriages and had painted the signal box inside and out. After their posts were made redundant in the September this left just the manager, Mr Crawley, and Engineer, Mr Gordon. Subsequently, however, Mrs Crawley and Mrs Short came back on a seasonal part-time basis. Mrs Short, who had started working on the railway in 1988, remains a familiar figure for passengers, running the platform operations and providing clerical support to the railway when it is operating.

In 1992, a rare opportunity arose to add to the rolling stock of the railway. The Broughton Moor Military depot in Cumbria was constructed in 1939 and an extensive narrow gauge railway system was built up on the 1,250 acre site, different sources quote 25 and/or 36 miles of 2 ft 6 in. gauge track - whichever is correct it was one of the largest narrow gauge railway systems in the country!

It was also a site of great secrecy being an ammunition dump and it was rare, if not impossible, for railway enthusiasts to be permitted access until near the time of final closure. Closure of the depot had seemed likely at various times, only for a further use to be identified. As a result, the large fleet of locomotives remained in use despite their age and with the exception of some acquisitions in 1976, without modern replacements. In 1981, the depot was given official NATO status, being now used by the United States Navy. A programme of modernisation was commenced by Messrs W. Hocking & Co. Ltd of Tongwynlais near Cardiff and a study commenced with a view to purchasing a new fleet of locomotives. On 19th June, 1991, however, it was announced that the US Navy would be leaving and the depot would close at the end of December 1992. All equipment was to be removed from the site by 30th September, 1992. The railway appears to have officially closed on 5th July, 1992, but by then all but five locomotives had left the site.

The result of the closure was that large quantities of rails, sleepers and a number of locomotives and rolling stock became available for sale, moreover, with the same gauge as Whipsnade, thus removing any need to spend money and effort on re-gauging. The equipment was grouped into 'lots' for sale by tender and Mr Crawley, together with Peter Denton the Secretary of the Zoological Society and the manager of the Welshpool & Llanfair Railway went to Broughton Moor to examine what was available. At this time very active consideration was being given to extending the Whipsnade Railway and first thoughts were to bid for rails and sleepers which would be used for the extension. In addition, there was a requirement for a small diesel to handle track maintenance trains, the large Fowlers being inconvenient and expensive to run for this purpose, and small wagons to avoid having to use the ex-Bowater's frames for non-passenger uses. Estimates were prepared for the cost of the equipment required and submitted to the ZSL but the sums involved were judged to be far too high, the needs of the animal collections being greater. No tender was therefore submitted. However, agreement was reached with the W&L, which did submit a successful bid for a Hunslet diesel locomotive and some wagons, that three of the wagons in their 'lot' would be sold on to Whipsnade. These three were flat wagons and they were delivered direct to Whipsnade in about June 1992, one of which was subsequently converted into a hopper wagon for track ballasting.   The requirement for a small diesel locomotive remained and Mr Crawley established that Messrs W. Hocking & Co. Ltd had acquired various suitable items. Approval was obtained for the purchase of a Ruston locomotive together with two box vans. The result was the arrival at Whipsnade of the locomotive 'Mr Bill', together with the two vans, one of which was subsequently converted into a brake van. This equipment is described with more detail in Chapter Eight.

In early 1994, the General Manager, Mr Crawley, left the railway leaving only one full-time employee, the Engineer, Mr Ian Gordon. Mr Gordon had first joined the railway on a part- time basis some seven years before, joining the full time staff in mid-1990 when he became Engineer and head driver. He now took over the reigns as acting General Manager for the start of the new season. In a pre-season report prepared at the end of March, *Superior* was the only locomotive in working order. *Chevallier* needed some attention and was back in operation for the start of the season, *Excelsior* had a damaged pressure gauge and in the event was not used during 1994 while being re-tubed. There were problems with *Hector* which were not likely to be resolved until after the Easter period, removal and repair of the cylinder heads being required. *Victor* was going to have to 'borrow' the batteries from *Hector*, but could not in any case be used for passenger trains due to the absence of vacuum braking equipment. By the peak season, however, both *Superior* and *Chevallier* were working and *Hector* was back in action. Overall the season was good and as the railway closed down for the winter thoughts turned to consolidation and improvement ready for the 25th Anniversary season in 1995.

Into 1995

Although the normal season for 1994 had ended, as has become the practice in recent years, the railway operated during the week leading up to Christmas, partly in conjunction with 'Santa's Grotto', a zoo promotion located in the children's farmyard. The 1994 Christmas Eve was particularly memorable as a clear, crisp winter's day with a frost on the ground. The steam and smoke rising in the still, clear air, the white covering on the ground, and the train crew wearing red and white 'Santa' hats left an unforgettable impression!

The 1995 year began with still just one permanent, full time, member of staff, the manager Ian Gordon, although he was assisted by Tony Button on a more or less full time, but not, permanent basis. In addition, Graham Tyler worked on the engineering side on a part time basis. Betty Short was also back on running days to run the platform side, assisted by additional part time staff as the season progressed and traffic increased. The spot re-sleepering programme continued after Christmas 1994, and the railway opened again in January during the school holidays - some further memorable days running occurred following snowfalls. The December and January trains were handled by *Superior*, and *Hector* (freshly re-painted) was available if required. The regular season started in April and *Chevallier* was given a steam test, which was successful, and subsequently used on some days for regular traffic, *Superior* and *Hector* handling other trains according to the numbers of people in the park. In the meantime work was proceeding slowly on the reassembly of *Excelsior* after passing her boiler test, the tank and cab being re-painted in the planned Oxford Blue. The fare for 1995 was set at £1.60 for adults, 80p for children.

The Whipsnade Education Department run a 'Saturday Club' for children, organising a day in the zoo along a theme, usually related to animals. On Saturday 29th April the theme was to be the railway. Considerable advance planning and effort was put in by the railway manager, assisted by railway staff and volunteers to provide an enjoyable day out for the children. In the event some 48 children turned up. The activities were centred on four 'bases' and after a train ride for all of the 'Saturday Club' members, the children were split up into four groups and rotated round the bases. These were: an 'assault course' in the playground beside the railway, a further trip round the line and a visit to the footplate of *Superior* which was in steam for the day, a simple talk about how steam locomotives work followed by the freedom to clamber all over *Chevallier* and *Hector* which were located on the south loop line in the station, and a painting competition using the panels of two carriages parked on the south loop between the crossing gates and the turnout. The latter two bases proved to be the most popular, with the children delighting in getting as dirty as possible, some venturing inside the firebox and smokebox of *Chevallier* (which was not in steam!). What started as two red carriages acquired a multi-coloured appearance, the like of which the railway had never before seen. Naturally considerable attention was paid to safety, each group being accompanied by both education and railway staff and volunteers equipped with radios, Section 6 of the line being a 'safety zone' which was cleared before the train was allowed to even enter the tunnel. The day was voted a great success and the railway won a lot of new friends, in fact it was decided to leave the decorated carriages as they were for the following weekend's annual 'Steam Up' in order that the children's painting efforts could be more widely seen.

The 'Steam up' weekend took place over the 6th, 7th and 8th May, 1995 with *Chevallier* and *Superior* in steam. Trains early in the day were run as double-headers, the two locomotives then operating a two-train service later to handle Bank Holiday crowds. This year it was decided not to run a 'goods' train as a special attraction. Another small break with the past was the departure of various items from the railway. Just before the 'Steam Up' weekend Soham signal box departed from its position stored on the old station platform bound for its new owner, thus bringing to a close an ambitious project which had never got beyond the planning stage. The box was apparently none the worse for having fallen off its timber plinths shortly before it was due to be collected! On 6th May a lorry also left the park loaded with the turntable parts and the spare set of wheels for *Conqueror*, and four ex-Bowaters' wagon frames were returned to the park on the completion of the deal to sell *Conqueror* (*see later*).

A change within the park which may affect the railway concerned the road priority for visitors. From the opening of the loose surface road within the deer park, visitors who drove their own cars inside the zoo had a choice of turning right off the park roads into, and through, Cut Throat and Valley Meadow, or continuing straight on past the flamingo pond, over the tunnel bridge and on round Woodfield paddock. At the beginning of 1995 the option to drive straight on was removed, the road being marked with 'No Entry' signs, and all traffic was directed through the deer park road. The concern from the point of view of the railway is that, as a result of car drivers already having driven through the same area as the animals, there is little incentive to take a train ride through substantially the same area, albeit by a slightly different route. The degree to which this affects the railway remains to be seen. Shortly after the 'Steam Up' weekend, a structural Engineer visited the railway and expressed some concern about the tunnel roof where the road passes over the railway, advising that it should only be used for light traffic. In view of the changed road system the use of the bridge by cars will be reduced considerably; however this does not deal with the zoo's double-deck bus which traverses the park, and certainly not the steam traction engines and rollers which rumble round the park over 'Steam

Up' weekend. Subsequent investigation seems to indicate the problem is not with the bridge itself, but simply the road surface over it.

Plans for the Future

The future for the railway looks secure at the present time, indeed it is considered an intregal part in the '10 Year Plan' currently being developed for the whole park, although a number of the earlier plans for expansion are either on hold or simply abandoned in the light of available finance. In the early part of 1994 the zoo received a proposal to purchase the railway which did receive consideration but did not proceed. The railway is run as a department within the zoo, working within a budget agreed at the start of the financial year together with all other cost centres within the park and is required to make a profit. The railway in itself represents a significant attraction within the total park operation and provides visitors with an arguably unique experience operating, as it does, with vintage steam locomotives and trains running through paddocks housing large numbers of wild animals.

The light of experience under the ownership of the Zoological Society, however, has led to a reappraisal of the likely requirements for the railway in the foreseeable future and has shown that there are not large sums available for capital investment. As a result, an advertisement appeared in the October 1994 issue of *Railway World* magazine offering for sale equipment which was now considered surplus to requirements. The most significant item for sale was *Conqueror*. This locomotive had not been in use since about 1983 and was known to require a lot of work and large sums of money to renovate and return to traffic. The high hopes of accomplishing this were now viewed as unachievable with the current resources of manpower and finance available. Before the advertisement was placed, discussions had taken place with the Welshpool & Llanfair Railway Society concerning the possibility of an exchange of *Conqueror* for their locomotive *Joan* but the W&L decided that the repair of *Conqueror* was too costly for them to undertake. The subsequent sale of *Conqueror* means that there are now only three steam locomotives available for service at the most, one of which is not actually owned by the railway. *Chevallier* remains in the ownership of Sir William McAlpine and remains at Whipsnade by way of an agreement which basically requires that she is kept in good running order. This leaves little margin for breakdown or major repairs to one of the remaining locomotives, although with the peak season compressed as it is into a comparatively short period in the year any major repairs should be possible to one engine during the off season period. The railway also has the diesel *Hector* which can assist with passenger traffic and, by fitting vacuum brakes to *Victor*, a second diesel would become available if required. Also offered for sale were the standard gauge 5-ton crane which was out of use in the yard, and the components for the turntable owned by the railway. This kit of parts was to construct a 32 ft 1 in. long turntable for 2 ft 6 in. gauge, although the gauge could easily be narrowed, or widened to metre gauge. The intention, it will be recalled, was to locate this in the yard and provide the capability to turn carriage stock to even out the wear bias caused by continuous running round the circuit. A number of enquiries were received about *Conqueror*, but the most promising discussion resulted in a deal being verbally agreed on the last day of September for the sale of *Conqueror* and the turntable in return for £12,000 and four Bowater's wagons. The Bowater's wagons had been sold with two others a few years earlier, their return would now provide a source of spares for the existing Whipsnade carriages and the capability of further construction if the need arose in the future.

The cash received will be available to spend on the railway and not taken into general zoo funds and a policy of steady and achievable progress is now being followed. Over the next two years the intention is to sort out and rationalise the current equipment and improve the facilities in the yard and old station area. The first step was taken at the end of the 1994 operating season with the start of work to create a new approach road from the 'farm' into the yard on the eastern side which will improve access for deliveries. Further work will represent a revised assessment of the plans drawn up in 1990 and the first visible progress will be the re-cladding of the shed (using the existing framework) following which it will be rewired, the new lathe installed and overall resulting in an improved environment for staff to maintain the locomotives. The grass bank between the railway main line and the old station just beyond the crossing needs to be stabilised and landscaped and the work may include the construction of a proper loading bay for road deliveries to the railway, making the handling of coal, fuel and other items a much easier task than at present. Further work planned in the yard area includes removal of the concrete under the track bed which causes problems in holding the track to alignment (presently assisted by wood planks nailed to the outer ends of the sleepers!), together with a realignment of the track in order to ease the tight curves, particularly the excessively sharp 'corner' from the signal box round to the exit from the yard into the woods. The condition of the track has been a source of comment for many years. Although the rails are sound, a large number of sleepers required replacement. During the summer of 1994, a number were replaced between the station and road crossing in the mornings before trains commenced. Through the winter of 1994/95, some 400 sleepers out on the circuit were replaced with newly-purchased material to produce a considerably improved permanent way for the 1995 season. A major event for 1995 will be the return to service of *Excelsior* after re-tubing, thus making all three steam locomotives available for service, and it is intended that the partially converted coach will also be completed, adding another high capacity coach to stock.

In the longer term, it is planned to add vacuum braking equipment to *Victor*, which will make a second diesel available for passenger services if required, followed by the conversion of all the presently piped only carriages to full vacuum braking. Some considerable renovation work is required to the coaching stock at present, at minimum a number will require work to the floors and they will probably acquire wood flooring, as has been done to some vehicles already. In addition, the return of the four Bowater's wagons will enable the construction of a further train of coaches as envisaged back in the 1990 General Manager's report if required.

As ever, the fortunes of the railway will be closely related to the number of visitors through the gates to the park itself. However,the railway can maximise the number of potential passengers by maintaining an efficient and intensive service at peak times. There is scope for additional numbers of trains and capacity if the potential passengers are there and the work being done is aimed at achieving this. The railway is also looking at ways in which it can raise income on its own account. At present, there are certainly some visitors who come to ride on the railway rather than to visit the zoo, and with the 25th anniversary of the first passenger train in August 1995 there should be a noticeable increase in the interest of enthusiasts in the railway. A further project which is being looked at is the introduction of steam driving courses. Such events have proved to be very well patronised, not to mention profitable, on preserved railways which have held them where, in return for a course fee, people receive both classroom and practical tuition in driving steam locomotives and, of course, turns on the regulator. Whipsnade provides an ideal site for such courses, not only does the circuit lend itself to such tuition by avoiding the frustration of 'out and back' trips for drivers together with the attraction of viewing the animals for course members between taking their turns on the footplate, but the park is easily accessible from London and the Midlands with little competition in the same catchment area.

Plans That Never Happened

Most, if not all, railways have plans and ideas for projects which, in the event, never occurred. Looking through archives to see 'what might have been' can be a fascinating experience and gives some insight to the ambitions of the lines' owners. These projects often include ambitions to extend the original railway, in the case of Whipsnade this happened very early in the life of the railway. A plan was mooted around 1975/76 which would have formed a five mile run taking in the Downs on the far side of the park and including five stations. This idea was dropped, one of the major problems being the conflict with cars near the zoo entrance. Unfortunately, no actual plan or map for this proposal has been traced. Further ideas about extending the railway arose in the mid-1980s and have been mentioned earlier; although the animal exhibits were moved around, the railway retained its existing route.

The next plan for an extension to the railway came up in early 1991. British Rail had asked Andrew Forbes, then the Chief Executive of Whipsnade, to produce a paper on the Whipsnade Railway. Frazer Crawley responded to Mr Forbes' request for background information on 8th April, 1991, with two memoranda. The first detailed track related items which may be surplus to BR requirements which Whipsnade could use, as well as suggesting the loan of a BR track gang and the donation of surplus station buildings and shelters. The second enclosed a plan for a 2 mile extension to the existing railway. The plan was for an enlarged continuous circuit with the new section a rough mirror image of the existing circuit. The new line would have left the existing track in Round Close and continued on a left handed curve across Lay Meadow, then right on entering Hallcraft. In Spicers field it would have paralleled the road, passed just to the north of the new white rhino house and then swung right to head back towards the two ponds in the centre of the zoo which house the seals and contain the squirrel monkeys, before re-entering Round Close and joining the existing route before the ha-ha and level crossing. Overlaid on this plan was an alternative route which would have taken the railway out onto the top of the Downs and would have offered spectacular views over the Vale of Aylesbury. A considerable amount of work continued on this plan and related items during 1991 and 1992. The intention was to purchase redundant rolling stock from Poland where it was found that passenger lines were to close at the end of October 1991. It was assumed that discussions on the proposals would take place into 1992, allowing construction to take place in the winter of 1992/93, with opening for public service at Easter 1993. Work proceeded on budgets, costings and even a paper on the benefits of appreciation of rolling stock assets was prepared, in comparison to the depreciation of the road train vehicles. This project was one of several proposals for Whipsnade which were included in the 1991 development plan for the park, but which later were considered not to be financially viable in circumstances applying at the time. The idea did not disappear completely, however.

Although no background paperwork has been traced, two maps showing slightly different route schemes have been found in the railway files. They are not dated but are believed to have been prepared in 1991/92 as a development of the earlier proposal prepared by Frazer Crawley. In both schemes, the route mileage would have been roughly doubled and become a figure of eight in shape. The existing circuit would have remained, but the tracks in the Round Close paddock would have been divided instead of connecting, as now. Following the circuit as at present, on leaving the tunnel the line would have continued more or less straight, with a new Central station near the seal pond. The track would then have continued to a point near the zoo entrance, then left towards the present white rhino paddock. Entering the rhino paddock would, of course, have recreated the original railway experience. On leaving the rhinos there would have been a new 'Africa station' with the line continuing in a leftward curve until reaching a 'South America station'. It would then have continued until crossing the outward part of the circuit at a right angle in Round Close (the Scheme Two plan shows this would have been by an overbridge) and joined up with the existing line before crossing Central Avenue as it does now. The plan appears to have been intended to include some seven stations and the result would probably have made the existing road based 'Trail Breaker' redundant, elevating the railway to the principal method of transport within the park for visitors who did not bring cars inside. In the end, all this work came to nothing, as so often before, but what a prospect it would have been!

Another plan for a possible railway extension was prepared by Frazer Crawley in January 1993. This was produced as an outline proposal and included very rough costings and was prepared in the event that the zoo's development manager found an opportunity to offer the project to a potential sponsor. This plan had a similar concept to those detailed previously with a route broadly similar, except that in Round Close there would have been a connection on the level achieved with two points, thus allowing the 'new' section to be traversed in either direction, still arriving back at Whipsnade Central facing the right way. This was in contrast to the first plan, which had a right angle crossing, and the 1991 proposal which had no connection at all. This time the section on the Downs was omitted, although part of that extension in the woods near the brown bears' enclosure was retained, the line now cutting back to meet the earlier proposal in the vicinity of the new white rhino house. A passing loop would have remained at Whipsnade Central and additional loops installed at three more locations: in the first animal paddock (the old rhino paddock), in the woods to the north of the brown bears' enclosure and about mid-way along Cut Throat Avenue. There would have been four new stations on the extension and two on the existing line (in addition to Whipsnade Central) and the plan was that as various parts of the park were developed, theme stations would be opened up as well. The extension would have been 3.5 km, making a continuous run with the existing line of 5.5 km and it was anticipated that the existing line would be relaid to the same standard as the new section. The service envisaged was for five trains at peak periods and this was to be met by purchasing at least two extra steam locomotives from abroad, along with closed coaches, and overhauling *Conqueror*. These would be supplemented by a diesel railcar. The 'Wine and Dine' train would also have been incorporated, a proposal which had already been made and is covered later. In addition to the extension, a museum style building was proposed for the old station area behind the animal care centre, together with other exhibits including the Soham signal box and a viewing gallery for the locomotive running shed. If this scheme had progressed it would not only have brought about an impressive railway, but a narrow gauge museum and exhibition centre of imposing proportions. The scheme was obviously produced by the railway's then manager in the hope of keeping the concept 'alive' in case the opportunity for such a development would arise again, rather than representing a specific proposal for discussion at this stage. It is interesting that the zoo management consider the extension proposals to be 'on hold' as opposed to totally abandoned, although such a scheme would be only a part of an integrated long term plan for the park.

In the mid-1980s, there was a proposal to build a restaurant in the rhino paddock which would have been served by the railway. The location is not totally clear from the railway papers and the zoo administration do not have any records to clarify the matter. It is believed that it may have been located just off the point of the retaining wall which projects into the paddock shortly before the road crossing, pedestrian access also being gained by a footbridge. It is possible that more than one site was projected since the implication of some of the estimates is that there would have been rail access only and that additional track would be involved, perhaps from a branch off the main line. Some notes imply it could have been located in the second paddock rather than the rhino paddock. The idea seems to have been fully costed, but clearly second thoughts prevailed. In any event, when the rhinos were moved away to the other side of the zoo the attraction would have been reduced and it is now very unlikely that such a scheme would be revived. A project which was under very active consideration in the early 1990s was for the provision of a special 'wine & dine' train. The intention was to have a very up-market set of coaches to provide dining and cocktail facilities while viewing the animals. In April 1991, it looked as though things were moving quickly forwards. The General Manager, Mr Crawley, asked two possible suppliers for specific proposals and was hoping to receive details by Easter with a view to delivery and commencement of use in the spring of 1992. At the same time, an internal memo (to the park catering people?) was seeking suitable menus based on 60 to 80 diners. The two manufacturers replied promptly. Carnforth Railway Restoration and Engineering Services (a division of Steamtown Railway Museum Ltd) sent a very detailed proposal in the form of a brochure and Steam Traction Ltd offered a proposal for 'Pullman' coaches with galley and cocktail lounge facilities. The concept originated in conjunction with the equally active plans at the time for a railway extension, diners being transported through Asia, Africa, South America, etc. The proposal could, however, have been implemented by constructing a siding or loop on the circuit as it stands, a locomotive taking the train out into the paddocks where it could be 'parked' while conventional passenger services continued round the circuit, returning for it later. One can certainly visualise the attraction of a train being taken out into the animal paddocks by a diesel in the evening after normal passenger services had ceased and left on the track for the duration of the meal. Such a service would surely be unique and although no work is presently being done on such a project, it is considered to be 'on hold' so it may yet be revived.

Many years before, there had been a plan to convert one of the coaches into a railcar. This was dropped, but in his October 1989 report, Mr Crawley had raised the possibility of a one-person operated diesel-electric railcar which would allow all year round operating, and was going to approach the local technical college as a possible student project. The idea re-surfaced in February 1992 when the railway was offered a fully overhauled diesel railcar from Poland. The vehicle was fully enclosed and heated and designed for one person operation. The first offer was for an outright purchase, then was followed up by a lease purchase agreement with monthly payments spread over 3 to 4 years. The attraction would be the ability to operate between October and March and even greater profits were envisaged following the opening of the 'World Pavilion' station. This later project was a plan for the park which is no longer considered viable. The railcar idea was not followed up because the zoo did not have the available capital at the time, although as a concept it was not completely rejected.

In any event, the offer of the railcar was not taken up, but the concept of an all weather, all year, simple to operate addition to the rolling stock surfaced again at the beginning of the following year. This time the proposal was quite different from anything which had come before. A company named Parry People Movers Ltd supplied a detailed proposal for the supply and operation of a 'Minitram'. The basic idea behind the vehicle is that it is powered by a flywheel in combination with a low voltage electric motor. When the vehicle is going downhill the flywheel receives energy which is then utilised to take the vehicle over uphill sections. To get the vehicle started in the mornings, or help it over climbs the flywheel cannot cope with, the electric motor comes into play, working either from an overnight charge or a low voltage conductor rail. The body of the 'Minitram' could either be supplied in the form of a reproduction of an old style tram or with a very modern looking small railcar design. It would have seated about 14 passengers. The proposal for Whipsnade would have involved installing a conductor rail in Whipsnade Central station and for 150 yards up the hill out of the station and in Round Close paddock to cope with the climb out of the tunnel. There would also have been a new shed in the yard to accommodate the vehicle equipped with an accumulator set for morning starting. The whole concept was based on a gauge of 2 ft 6 in. or thereabouts and one of the main promoters of the system was based in Milton Keynes and wanted a test installation close to their area. The manufacturers, however, did not agree and the cost quoted on a commercial basis was far beyond the resources available at Whipsnade and the idea was dropped without really coming very close to fruition.

There is an intriguing element to the proposal for the 'Minitram' in that the manufacturer's proposal supplied in May 1993 included the statement '. . . concept for putting down new stretches of railway to cover other areas is equally interesting.' Clearly, the earlier ambitions for expanding the route of the railway had not completely died away even by then.

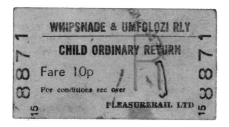

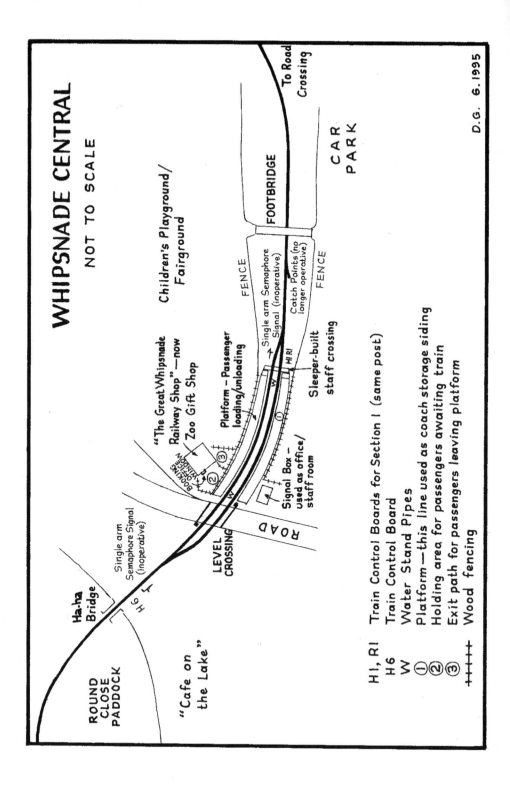

WHIPSNADE CENTRAL

NOT TO SCALE

ROUND CLOSE PADDOCK

"Cafe on the Lake"

Ha-ha Bridge

H 6

Single arm Semaphore Signal (inoperative)

"The Great Whipsnade Railway Shop" —now Zoo Gift Shop

BOOKING OFFICE WINDOW

③
②

LEVEL CROSSING

W

Platform – Passenger loading/unloading

Children's Playground / Fairground

W

Signal Box – used as office/ staff room

ROAD

①

H1 R1

Single arm Semaphore Signal (inoperative)

FENCE

Catch Points (no longer operative)

Sleeper-built staff crossing

FENCE

FOOTBRIDGE

To Road Crossing

CAR PARK

H1, R1 — Train Control Boards for Section 1 (same post)
H6 — Train Control Board
W — Water Stand Pipes
① — Platform – this line used as coach storage siding
② — Holding area for passengers awaiting train
③ — Exit path for passengers leaving platform
+++++ — Wood fencing

D.G. 6.1995

Victor waits with a train at Mulobezi Halt in 1975. Passengers could walk across the prepared area on the top of the bank and down the steps to the Zambezi Sawmills display, in the foreground are the automatic barrier lights to protect the road crossing. *Nick Robey*

After passing under Cut Throat Avenue the line enters Round Close paddock, the tunnel on this side being finished with a brick portal which incorporates a viewing platform and telescope above. *Author*

The original track stopped in the upper part of this view. When the line was extended the rails were continued into a curve and across this new ha-ha (the second on the circuit) which divided the Rhino paddock from Valley Meadow. Umfolozi Halt was built on the left of the line a few yards on from the bottom of the picture.

Author

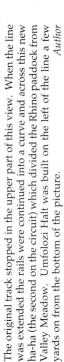

The track leaves Round Close paddock (upper part of the picture) and crosses the last ha-ha shortly before crossing Central Avenue and entering the station. Note that the ha-ha's differ in design from each other, this having brick facing to the supports.

Author

Superior is passing the site of the old station, the access to which was down the slope centre-right. Just visible behind the last coach are the remains of the sleeper fronted platform of Mulobezi Halt. *Author*

The railway Manager and Engineer, Ian Gordon, prepares *Superior* for a day's work in April 1995, *Excelsior* is just visible inside the shed - not yet re-assembled after receiving new tubes. *Author*

The interior of the cab of *Superior*.

Author

Excelsior and her train surrounded by white rhino on 27th July, 1977.

Zoological Society of London

Excelsior outside the engine shed in about 1974.

Graeme Carr

Excelsior inside the shed late in 1994 following the re-tubing work.   *Author*

Pictured in 1971, possibly 1972, *Conqueror* brings a train into the old north platform at the original station. The locomotive is in the original green livery at this time.   *Trevor Barber*

Conqueror in the south platform of the original station, probably in 1971. The bushes visible behind and to the left mark the boundary of what was then the children's zoo.   *Trevor Barber*

Pictured in the yard, *Superior* is in green livery as she arrived at the railway. Just visible to the right and on the siding behind is the Motor Rail diesel. *Trevor Barber*

The first steaming of *Superior* in June 1974 following extensive overhaul and displaying the brand new paint scheme. *Martin Johnson*

Chapter Six

The Route Described

Track Marker Boards

There are section marker boards beside the track all round the circuit. Their locations are identified in the following descriptions of the route. For details of the method of train control relating to the markers refer to Chapter Seven - 'Working the Line.'

Whipsnade Central Station & Buildings

The railway technically has two stations but, in reality, the terminus, Whipsnade Central, is the only station used. The western limit of the station is defined by the level crossing where the railway crosses Central Avenue almost at right angles, and the eastern end by the ends of the platforms and marker boards H1 and R1. The road across the crossing is concrete and is protected by two metal gates, each hinged from opposite sides of the railway. The gates are painted cream and have red 'targets' in the centres. On the north side of the railway beside the gates is 'The Great Whipsnade Railway Shop'. The exterior is of varnished wood, the flat roof is finished with red fascia boarding, below which is a decorative yellow plastic finishing piece with ornate frets cut into the bottom edge. The shop is a conventional zoo gift shop, but let into the outside face of the back wall is a booking office window and the wall facing the road has a board giving the times between which trains will be running and the fares payable. Having purchased tickets, passengers proceed up a short path, through a gate in the fence which surrounds the whole station site, and onto the platform.

The track layout in the station is of a simple loop, the western turnout for which is on the other side of Central Avenue, thus the crossing is apparently double tracked. The eastern turnout is beyond the platform ends, adjacent to the semaphore signal. The track through the station is on a curve and the platforms naturally follow this. The main line is on the north (shop) side, the loop being on the south (signal box) side. The platforms are brick faced, the surface being concrete with a white edge. The only building on the south side of the line is a small signal box. This now forms a staff rest room and storage area with a small office at one end for the manager and Engineer. The building is painted in juniper and cream and the front is decorated by hanging flower baskets along with a flower planter formed from railway sleepers; other similar planters are located on the platforms. Both sides of the platforms are adorned with vintage lamp standards and railway seats.

At each end of the platform length, located between the tracks, is a standpipe connected to a mains water supply and at the east end of the platforms wooden sleepers provide a pedestrian crossing for the use of staff.

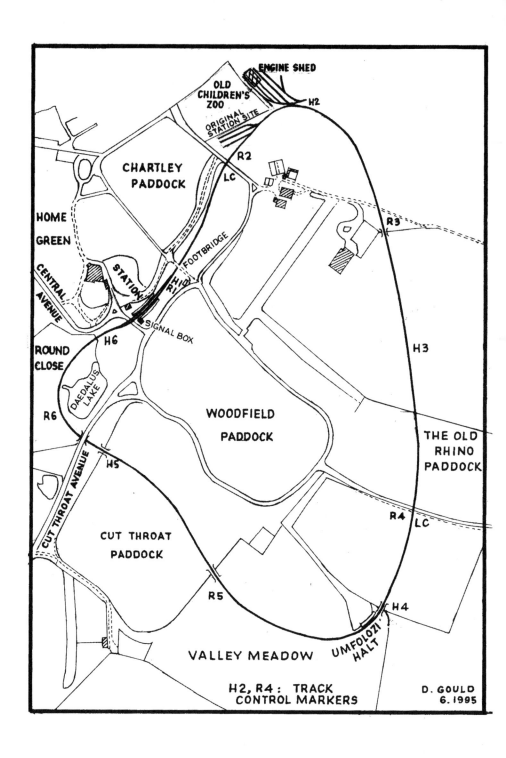

ENGINE SHED

OLD CHILDREN'S ZOO

ORIGINAL STATION SITE

H2

R2

LC

CHARTLEY PADDOCK

HOME GREEN

CENTRAL AVENUE

STATION

FOOTBRIDGE

HIGH R1

SIGNAL BOX

R3

H6

ROUND CLOSE

DAEDALUS LAKE

R6

WOODFIELD PADDOCK

H3

THE OLD RHINO PADDOCK

CUT THROAT AVENUE

H5

CUT THROAT PADDOCK

R4 LC

R5

H4

VALLEY MEADOW

UMFOLOZI HALT

H2, R4 : TRACK CONTROL MARKERS

D. GOULD 6. 1995

Trip Round the Line

As the train sits in the station, to the right is grass and a road parallel to the railway. Across from this behind the trees and shrubs is the fenced off tiger enclosure and 'Tiger Falls'. On the left is a children's playground and a small fairground. As the train leaves the station, the land level on each side of the line rises and the railway is running in a shallow grass-sided cutting. Shortly, the railway crosses a catch point with a small 'Catch point' notice to the left of the track (required originally in the days before vacuum brakes were fitted to prevent runaways detached from a departing train from coming back down the gradient and re-entering the station), and passes under a pedestrian footbridge. The bridge is formed by three sections of heavy steel girder on each side to give the two ascending angles and flat top section. The treads (steps) are of wood planks and metal railings are attached to the girders on each side. The bases of the bridge on each side are formed from the same grey bricks as are used for the exit from the tunnel. On the right hand side is a car park and on the left is a grass field attached to the children's farmyard, which often results in seeing animals as diverse as sheep, cows and camels close to the fence! This is followed by the 'Bear Trail', a display which does not house live bears! At this point the line is climbing and in damp weather the first train of the day can have problems with slipping.

The track swings to the left and then back right and a marker board on the right of the tracks can be seen. This is a white board with a large figure '8' above the instruction 'whistle', both picked out in black. The locomotive slows and duly sounds the whistle as the line passes a colour light signal and crosses the road on the level. This crossing is protected by an automatic device triggered by the passing wheels of the locomotive. An audible warning sounds and a red light is shown to road users, at the same time the railway signal which normally shows the default red switches to green clearing the train to proceed. The road used also to be protected by a single arm barrier on the left of the crossing, the arm was removed when the one-way direction for road traffic was changed. The unit was not moved to the other side of the junction, partly because it had been known to catch car drivers who were not expecting it to lower! Now, a notice (black lettering on white board) states 'Automatic Controls (No Barriers) Stop When Lights Show', and there are international railway crossing signs. These notices are on both sides of the road although it is supposed to be one-way only - internal zoo vehicles do not necessarily follow the one-way system applicable to visitors. On crossing the road, the railway swings gently to the right, passing on the left side a grass bank retained by a rough wall of old sleepers (the site of the old Mulobezi Halt) and on the left a colour light signal and 'whistle' board which face in the opposite direction. These duplicate those on the other side and are for the use of a train, or locomotive, travelling from the yard to Whipsnade Central, there being a duplicate automatic trigger device for the rail and road lights on this side of the crossing. On the right of the tracks is marker 'R2'.

The gradient levels over the road crossing and starts to descend, the train now beginning to drift on the downgrade. On the left can be seen the site of the original terminus, followed by the loco coal stack, water tower, a white wooden building which was also a signal box and known in the early years as Whipsnade Junction signal box, then the engine shed and yard. On the right the line passes a single white crossing gate and curving to the right skirts a grass bank and runs past a double arm semaphore signal and the remaining sidings. A few yards after the signal is marker 'H2' on the right of the tracks. The yard and old station are described separately later.

At this point it is possible to see over to the left the animal care centre where orphaned animals are taken for hand rearing, also the crane breeding centre which is not accessible to the public since the birds need privacy to breed (nine species of endangered cranes have been bred at Whipsnade). Continuing to curve to the right, the line enters a small wood and straightens out, the gradient remains downward and the driver controls the train on the brake rather than the regulator. To the left are fields which are part of the zoo and passengers will see wallaby and Chinese water deer if they keep a lookout. The locomotive whistles again as the train approaches another level crossing. This time the road is an unmade zoo service track with simple gates which, if closed to the railway, the fireman has to go forward and open. The line is now on a completely straight stretch. Shortly after, the crossing marker 'R3' on the right of the line is passed and the track immediately crosses the first ha-ha into the animal paddocks. This ha-ha is a single span, the bridge part being two steel girders supporting a rail on each. The girders are connected horizontally by steel cross pieces, and these are braced by a series of steel angle strips secured at 45° between the ends of each consecutive cross piece. The inner (paddock) side of the ditch is protected by a ring of log stumps set vertically into the ground. Although the smaller animals pass between these they cannot escape out of the ditch due to the resultant height of the wire link fence which continues across the top of the outer support. No animal would be capable of crossing the bridge since the gaps are considerably wider than a conventional cattle grid.

A large building to the right is the old white rhino house, now used to accommodate the camels. Looking across the grass to the right can be seen a construction of some length reminiscent of a stockade! Far from being the remains of an old fort, this is the result of the construction of a clear view area for the visitors to see the animals living in the paddock which originally included white rhino and wildebeest. The surface of the paddock dips down into a shallow ditch from which a bank was then built up at a sharp angle and faced with vertical timber to hold the bank in place. The animals could not get up the bank from the ditch and no fences or wire were needed in front of the people. Beyond the bank and just behind a line of trees are separate accommodation and enclosures for gaur and Indian rhinoceros. A section of the grass back to the right is divided from the main paddock by a light electrified fence. This area is available for another Indian rhinoceros which used to be allowed to roam the main paddock but tended to chase the cars, to the understandable consternation of the visitors! The bank juts out into the paddock to form a viewing point and near the closest point to the railway, marker 'H3' is passed on the right.

For the rest of the trip the railway will be surrounded on all sides by animals free to roam on the extensive, undulating grasslands. Despite the size of the paddocks, the different species of animals not only tend to stay in their own groups, but the areas in which they tend to be seen are surprisingly consistent. This first paddock normally houses Pere David's deer, yak and bactrian camels, also mara which live free all over the park, but the first section of this paddock is the most likely place to be able to see the very small baby mara at the top of their burrows.

Shortly after 'H3' the line swings to the right, then straightens as a board on the right is passed. This is a white board with an 'X' above the figure '8'. The cross, figure and surrounding edge of the board are black. This sign warns of the forthcoming road crossing and reminds the driver of the 8 mph speed limit. The road is used by visitors driving their own cars through the upper part of Cut Throat paddock and Valley Meadow, an recent innovation which allows different views of the animals of Asia, together with good views in several places of the passing trains. The crossing between road and rail is at right angles, the actual crossing being a concrete pad as opposed to the loose surface of the rest of the road. Car drivers are warned on both sides of the crossing (even though the road route is one-way) to 'Give Way' and 'Keep Crossing Clear' by conventional road signs, the message being reinforced by two international signs for a railway crossing. The amount of road traffic is not a problem for the railway, a more likely cause for hold ups being the presence of yak and camels, both of which tend to gather in this area encouraged by the heaps of hay put down for them by the keeping staff together with a small water hole at which the animals can drink. The direction of travel for the road is from left to right and the road continues in a straight line to a car park visible further over to the right. Immediately after the crossing, marker 'R4' is located to the right of the line. On looking back, a railway sign for a train travelling anti-clockwise can be seen. This sign does not duplicate that for the normal direction of travel, being a large white board with a red circle above the black lettering 'Stop - Check Crossing Clear Whistle Before Proceeding', the difference being that only works trains would be likely to work in an anti-clockwise direction. The area on the right of the train bounded by railway, road and the adjacent paddock fence is the area where one is most likely to see the impressive herd of Pere David's deer.

The straight section of line we have been on now gives way to a long curve to the right. The line straightens slightly and crosses a small pedestrian type level crossing, swings right again and across the second ha-ha. The metalwork is of similar design to the previous ha-ha but the ditch is much wider, thus the rails are supported by a central supporting pier of stone blocks resulting in a two span bridge. The fence dividing the paddocks meets the central pier along the middle of the bottom of the ditch which tends to be water filled. As soon as the train comes off the bridge and regains the land surface level there is a construction of railway sleepers supported by metal uprights driven into the ground. This is the site of Umfolozi Halt. The halt was built in 1974 and in 1992 the construction remained complete. By 1994, however, a number of the sleepers had been removed and the halt is now very dilapidated. The platform was at the correct height for entering and leaving the coaches and consisted of large timber balks laying at right angles to the railway supported on two 'walls' of sleepers. Only about five of the platform timbers remain, but the site officially retains the status of being a station - trains do not stop and passengers are not encouraged to alight, however! The halt has never been used for passengers to join or alight from a train, it did however provide a means of escape from the paddocks if a train encountered difficulties. There used to be a double fence between the adjacent paddocks forming a path back to the road. Beside the halt is marker 'H4'.

The railway is paralleled by a wire link fence a few feet from the rails on the right hand side which separates further enclosures from the railway and the main paddock. The animals in the first enclosure here are onager. The main paddock is very large and with rolling grasslands sweeping away behind, upwards to the left, and away in front of the train. This paddock contains blackbuck, nilgai, axis deer, sika deer, hog deer and fallow deer. Away to the left of the train is the waterhole where animals will be drinking or wading out into the small lake. The railway curves to the right and follows the line of the fence through almost all of the remaining distance in this paddock. Higher up the slope on the left can be seen the 'Passage through Asia' road. On these slopes are likely to be groups of hog deer and fallow deer, the male blackbuck are also often to be seen either here or back towards the water hole. While travelling along this section train crews sometimes encounter animals which are between the rails and the fence and which appear completely unable to decide whether to go forwards or back, but crossing the line back onto the grass does not seem to be an option they consider. Invariably these will be nilgai, since this group tends to be seen at this end of the paddock (although it should be noted that occasionally species are moved around the paddocks and can vary from those quoted). Clearly, when confronted by a steam locomotive, the animals of Asia behave no differently from the sheep of Wales!

Although the line is beginning to climb mid-way along this section, this does not result in any problems. The train crews are used to this and slow, or stop if necessary, and the animals eventually move away from the line allowing the train to proceed. The open enclosures on the right now become woodlands and marker 'R5' is passed, followed by a curve to the right then a bridge over a culverted stream. This is not, strictly speaking, a ha-ha since it does not separate two paddocks. The construction is in the form of a small double span bridge, the ends and centre pier being built from stone, the rails being supported on two large steel girders. The girders are of one length, resting in recesses let into the top of the central pier, the rails being at the height of the top of the pier. There is no cross bracing as on the two ha-has already crossed. Passing over the bridge, the railway proceeds in a straight line and crosses open grass fields, the fence and edge of the woods angling back away to the right. The onager enclosure ends and most of the wooded area on the right is a separate enclosure occupied by blackbuck, normally females, the adolescent and mature males roam in the main area shared with the railway. The line then curves to the left, passes one of the animal shelters and straightens out as it enters a grass sided cutting. The gradient increases and the sides of the cutting become steadily higher as the railway approaches the tunnel and passes marker 'H5'. Just before entering the tunnel the line crosses another ha-ha which marks the end of this paddock. This has another double span bridge of similar, but larger, construction to the culvert bridge with the rails supported on girders recessed into the central pier and no cross bracing steel work, there are also metal plates set on top of the stonework of the three piers. The ditch here is completely filled with water, almost to the bottom of the crossing girders. The railway now commences a long right curve as it enters the tunnel.

This is initially a concrete sided cutting with girders over the train between the top coping of the vertical walls to hold them apart at the correct distance. It then becomes a bridge carrying a road over the line. A sharp lookout is required by both members of the locomotive crew since it is possible, and known, for animals to enter the tunnel, at times even being seen on the bank beside the water filled ditch at the entrance. The entire construction is on a curve giving restricted vision and clearances, plus an up gradient - as if the driver did not have enough to contend with! The far end of the tunnel is built from grey brick, the exit being constructed with an observation platform equipped with a telescope above. Brick-built retaining walls hold the grass embankment which leads up to the level of the road above. Accompanied by much whistling, the train clears the tunnel and continues its right curve passing marker 'R6' on the right hand side. It is worth mentioning that the board for this marker is often turned, or comes off the post completely. This is because the swamp deer find it very convenient to rub against - such are the problems of railway operation when the route is shared with large animals!

To the left of the train is open grass paddock, to the right is Daedalus Lake, so named because men from the Royal Navy shore base HMS Daedalus helped with its construction. The paddock normally houses barasingha (also called swamp deer) and barhead geese along with various ducks. The lake has small islands within it and contains carp, although the water is not very deep. The locomotive is now working hard up a 1 in 24 climb, the line still on a right curve. To the right on the far side of the fence is an aviary housing scarlet ibis, beside which can be seen the lakeside cafe which has picnic tables outside on the grass offering a pleasant view for visitors taking refreshments. During the winter of 1994/95 this cafe was extensively re-built and expanded in order to become the principal catering facility in the park. The railway now crosses the last ha-ha on the circuit. This is a single span bridge with the rails supported on steel girders let into the support piers and a pipe is also carried across the ditch on the centre line between the girders. The piers themselves are faced with similar grey bricks to those used on the tunnel exit and the perimeter fence abuts the far pier. On the right beside the line is marker 'H6'. The line then moves over a point, normally taking the left line, passes a semaphore signal on the right, and on a slightly left curve crosses Central Avenue to arrive back at Whipsnade Central station.

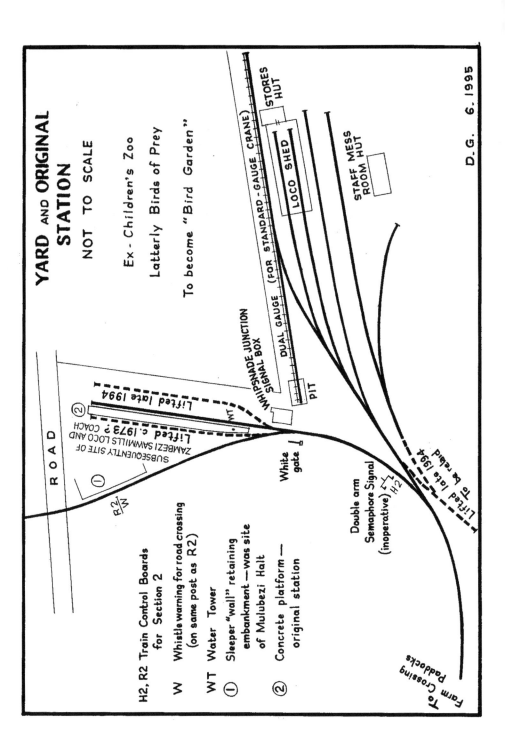

YARD AND ORIGINAL STATION

NOT TO SCALE

Ex - Children's Zoo

Latterly Birds of Prey

To become "Bird Garden"

H2, R2 Train Control Boards for Section 2

W   Whistle warning for road crossing (on same post as R2)

WT Water Tower

① Sleeper "wall" retaining embankment — was site of Mulubezi Halt

② Concrete platform — original station

ROAD

R2/W

SUBSEQUENTLY SITE OF ZAMBEZI SAWMILLS LOCO AND Lifted c. 1973 ? COACH

①

②

Lifted late 1994

WHIPSNADE JUNCTION SIGNAL BOX

DUAL GAUGE (FOR STANDARD-GAUGE CRANE)

STORES HUT

LOCO SHED

STAFF MESS ROOM HUT

PIT

White gate

Lifted late 1994 to be relaid

Double arm Semaphore Signal (inoperative) H2

To Farm Crossing Paddocks

D.G. 6. 1995

Yard and Sidings (incl. Buildings)

The following sites are all visible from the left side of the train shortly after it passes the level crossing over the first road upon leaving Whipsnade Central station. The public, however, are not allowed access to any parts of the zoo in the following description.

The track layout in the yard falls into two sections. The first is the site of the original station built for the opening of the railway when it was a simple out and back line. It ceased to be used as a station when the new Whipsnade Central was built. A trailing point just before the white signal box on the left of the main line leads back into the old station down the north side of a low, but clearly raised, concrete platform and is used for rolling stock storage. A second turnout formed another siding parallel to the platform line beside the fence which surrounds the old children's zoo. This siding was lifted at the end of October/beginning of November 1994. There used to be a second station line on the other (main line) side of the platform but these tracks were lifted some years ago. For a time after the extension of the railway into a full circuit this side of the platform was used to display 3 ft 6 in. stock from the Zambezi Sawmill Railway (*see Chapter 5*).

The platform is now empty, but was used to store Soham signal box, supported on plinths of timber and old sleepers awaiting a decision as to its future use. At the main line end of the platform is the water tower which consists of a large cylindrical tank mounted on top of a girder and angle built supporting frame. Almost beside the water tower and spread over what was once the throat of the other platform line is the coal heap for the steam locomotives. There is a sleeper built foot crossing for staff which crosses from the platform over the remaining two sidings towards the Whipsnade Railway's signal box located on the north side of the main line at the corner of the site formed by the children's zoo. This building is used for storage. Almost opposite the signal box is a white painted level crossing gate mounted at the bottom of the grass bank on the other side of the main line. The purpose of the gate is now unclear but the intention could have been that in the early days, by closing the gate, the end of what was then the station could have been closed off to prevent passengers wandering up the line towards the animal paddocks or into the yard proper. A very unusual feature around this section of the yard, including the main line, is the presence of wood boards which are secured to the top of the outer ends of the sleepers. These form very convenient walkways for staff walking down the line, but their real purpose is to reinforce the track location. Part of the track formation on the section in the vicinity of the signal box is actually located on a concrete bed (an extension of the alterations made in the old station site to counter subsidence of the track formation) and, despite conventional ballasting, the track is not all that firmly embedded as it would be on a normal ground surface. The boards help to lock the relative positions of the sleepers, and thus the rails, into the correct position. Behind the signal box the fence of the children's zoo site turns at a right angle and forms the limit of the site of the main yard. The children's zoo was closed when the facility was replaced by the children's farmyard which was built on the other side of the main road. The site is now used to house the birds of prey, along with macaws and parakeets, the birds being seen in the free flying displays held in the park. This area had not been open to the public for some time, but following alterations during the winter of 1994/95 the area was opened up by Easter 1995 and is being developed as a bird garden.

The main yard consists of a fan of sidings accessed from a trailing point off the main line located further round the right-handed curve just beyond the 'H2' marker board. A few yards before the 'H2' board, on the right of the main line, is a double arm semaphore signal mounted on a single post. The intention would have been for one signal to control the main line and the other the line into the yard joining from the left, but in fact this was never operational. For the purposes of clarity of description is would be simplest to assume one has moved beyond the point and is now reversing back into the yard!

The first turnout is a trailing point leading to a headshunt which runs back on the right, parallel to the main line. The headshunt itself was built on a gradient so that the end was actually somewhat higher than the main line beside it. However, at the end of October 1994, the track was lifted in connection with the construction of a new access road to the yard from the zoo 'farm'. When the road is completed the intention is to relay the track to the same arrangement but but on the same level as the adjacent lines, the new headshunt will also be somewhat longer than it was previously. The headshunt had a further turnout immediately after its own access point which led forwards, with a right bend, to run parallel to the other yard roads. Just after the bend in this siding is another turnout to a siding which peters out in the grass and appears to be no longer used. Towards the end of the main siding is a wooden shed located at an angle to the tracks which is used as a rest room for railway staff and can be used for some office paper work by the railway's Engineer.

Returning to the original 'main' siding turnout, after the headshunt turnout the line is straight but with three consecutive turnouts to the right leading into sidings which are parallel to each other. The first is a straightforward siding which runs down the east side of the engine shed, ending just short of the end of the shed building. The next two are the actual engine shed roads leading through the doors into the shed itself. After the shed roads the 'main' siding also turns to the right and runs down the far (west) side of the shed parallel with the shed wall and fence of the children's zoo. As this siding turns right to round the shed there is a trailing point which leads back into a short headshunt which terminates over a pit. On the face of it, this is a strange place for a pit to be located, since not only is it in the open (there is no evidence of having been covered over) but it would require two changes of direction for a locomotive to come out of the shed and stop over the pit and a further reverse and movement forward to leave the pit and return to the main shed road. Part of the explanation may lay in the presence of a third rail on the outside (west) of the headshunt which continues right down the side of the children's zoo fence to the far end of the siding at the back of the engine shed. This third rail forms a standard gauge line with the shed side rail of the 2 ft 6 in. track upon which stands the crane. This would allow for the crane to collect heavy items from the road access behind the shed and move them up to the headshunt where heavy work could be performed around or over the pit, there being no other means of achieving the movement of heavy items into the shed itself. The locomotive *Conqueror* which came out of service in 1983, was initially kept in the siding on the other side of the shed and latterly moved onto the rails over the pit, until November 1994 when the locomotive was moved into the old station ready for removal following its sale.

Interestingly, the standard gauge rail means that within the confines of the railway yard there have been a total of three different gauges over the years, albeit over very short distances!

The locomotive shed itself is a large building of wood construction, the sides being of horizontal timber planks attached to an internal frame. The original drawing dated 6th December, 1971, shows the dimensions to be 60 ft long by 23 ft 6 in. wide. The roof is ridged and formed of corrugated sheets, the ceiling inside is of wood planks supported on metal cross frames which traverse the shed from the top of the walls, and there are no smoke vents in the roof. There are square windows periodically down the west wall but none on any other wall, resulting in very poor natural light, supplemented by fluorescent tubes hanging from the ceiling. The front of the shed has similar wood planks from the top of the sides up to the ridge, below this line the front and doors are constructed from rather crude wood sheeting. Locomotives enter the shed through two large doors which have frames of metal angle and are sheeted in with panels similar to the rest of the front of the shed. The left door as one faces the shed has a small door for access by staff. The shed can accommodate four locomotives, two on each road, and at the back there is room for a lathe and workbench. Although it will retain the same basic shape, the shed is due to be reclad and will then be rewired to improve the internal electricity supply. Work was about to commence in early 1995, but as soon as the scaffolding was erected and men appeared on the roof, a number of birds in the bird of prey centre next door became distressed. The work was halted and by April 1995 a temporary screen was being put up and it is hoped that work will re-commence without disturbance to the birds. Such are the special problems confronting a railway in such an unusual location! A door in the back wall of the shed leads into another building. This is, in effect, a large wooden shed with a ridge roof which butts up to the back wall of the engine shed, but is located off centre to the engine shed, the west side projecting beyond the line of the engine shed wall, the other side being well short of the east wall. This extension was a McAlpine site hut and was added in about 1991 or 1992. The first room which is entered from the back of the engine shed is a workshop, suitable for painting and other general work, since it has windows down the right wall and is well lit in comparison with the very murky depths of the engine shed. Opening off to the left is a room used for stores.

Chapter Seven

Operating the Railway

Passenger Handling

The railway carries roughly a quarter of the total number of zoo visitors, so the number of passengers bears close relationship to the number of zoo visitors on any day. The percentage carried rises slightly if the calculation is made against visitors on days the railway is operating only, rather than across the year, although the difference is not all that great because, logically, the railway is open when there are large numbers of people in the park. The number of visitors to the park in winter is actually very small. The trend in the last few years does show that the percentage of visitors carried is rising and is, in some respects, a more accurate gauge of the popularity of the railway than the absolute numbers carried.

On the north side of the station beside the level crossing gates is 'The Great Whipsnade Railway Shop' and railway tickets are sold from a booking office window in the back wall beside the road. Passengers often arrive after the end of the sea lion show which is held a short distance away and a queue can quickly build up. A short path leads from the side of the shop up to the platform and passengers queue at the top of the slope behind gates in the fence. Passengers are not allowed to wait on the platform for a train. An arriving train will be unloaded and the platform cleared before passengers for the next are allowed through the gate from the 'holding area'. When the station staff are ready to allow passengers through onto the platform, the gate is opened, passengers show their tickets which are torn to cancel them and they are then allowed onto the platform to take their seats. When the train is ready for departure, the platform staff move along the train securing the coach doors and the train is cleared to depart.

When possible, normally during school holidays and at other peak times, a third person will make up the train crew. This is a zoo park volunteer who sits at the front of the leading coach and provides a commentary over a loudspeaker system throughout the train, covering the park, conservation efforts and describing animals which can be seen from the train, together with some details about the railway and the names of the locomotive and driver for the trip. There is a basic script for the commentary provided by the zoo education department but this is intended as a guide, the experienced volunteers quickly develop their own commentaries and style. The author recalls one occasion when the diesel engine *Hector* was having difficulty maintaining vacuum and the brakes came on in the yard. The volunteer maintained a commentary for over ten minutes while fitters worked to clear the problem, the trip having only just started and no animals had yet been seen! The depth of their knowledge can be immense. For instance, Lucy Pendar, whose father was the first Resident Engineer at Whipsnade, spent much of her childhood in the park and probably knows it better than anyone else (her book 'Whipsnade - My Africa' is highly recommended), and Hans Van Der Grinten whose infectious enthusiasm and humour has been known to result in applause from passengers as the journey ends. Credit is also due to all the other 'Vols' who add to the enjoyment of the trip for passengers.

At the end of the trip the station staff move down the platform undoing the doors and passengers leave the platform through a gap in the station fence which is roped across until a train arrives, then down a path which leads along the playground side of the shop.

There is no operating timetable - the first train departs at 12.30 pm during school holidays, 1.00 pm at other times, and trains will then be run as required depending on ticket sales and the length of the queue. Peak season operation is very intense with trains circulating continuously. For example, on 2nd May, 1994, a 'Steam Up Weekend' was held in the park with traction engines and other special attractions. The railway operated 44 trains in the day and carried 3,500 people, 23 trips were operated by *Superior* and 21 by *Chevallier*. A Bank Holiday Monday in 1994 saw 35 trains in a day, 20 worked by steam and 15 by diesel. Perhaps a more typical day in the summer holidays would see twelve trains a day, and by the end of season 1994 operations had reduced to just five diesel operated trains a day, each of these very lightly loaded, some trips carrying perhaps a dozen passengers. Normally the minimum number of passengers to make operating a train worthwhile is considered to be six.

Working the Line

The methods of operating the railway have become established over the years and have not changed greatly. Service trains travel in a clockwise direction, as has been the practise for many years, thus locomotives run chimney first at the head of their trains. It is feasible to run the other way round, and has been done on occasion, but is not desirable. Not only are the marker boards set up for clockwise running, but running anti-clockwise results in arrival at the station on a downgrade - and there is no margin for error with the crossing gates located at the end of the platforms! The only time a locomotive will run in reverse is when it is brought down from the shed to the station where it couples up to the coaches left in the station lines overnight. At Whipsnade Central the track on the north side of the station (playground side) is considered the main, the south (signal box) side being treated as the loop line. Both lines in the station are used for coach storage, both overnight during the season and throughout the winter. The carriage shed which was hoped for in the yard at the time the zoo took over has never been built. This also means that works trains are obliged to work out and back from the yard, almost traversing the full circuit if they are needed in the Round Close paddock, since there is no free road in the station. During peak operating, complete sets of coaches will be operating with locomotives, all arrivals and departures being handled on the north platform. When only one train is in use a rake of coaches will remain on the south side of the loop. This allows the locomotive to detach from its train, run forward across the loop point and then back to pick up another coach which is shunted onto the front of the train if additional capacity is needed. The only other exceptions to clockwise running will be for new drivers under instruction when a locomotive will have left the yard and entered the paddocks and returns in reverse rather than continuing right round the circuit.

Although there are three semaphore signals, two at Whipsnade Central apparently controlling the entrance to the station and departure onto the circuit, and a double arm signal in the yard, none of these are in operational use. All train control is by voice instruction and there is no necessity for staff, token or ticket control to give possession of the line. When only one engine is in steam (or diesel!) the train moves off when loaded and no further control is needed until it reaches the 'tunnel', whereupon it's whistles not only warn the animals of its approach, but call for the crossing gates at Central Avenue to be opened to allow entry to the station. Stopping on this section is not difficult, but highly unwelcome for a locomotive train crew faced with re-starting a heavily loaded train on the 1 in 24 gradient on a sharp curve!

During peak operating, when more than one train is working on the line, control is maintained by radio link between the locomotive crews and the controller in the signal box at Whipsnade Central. The use of radios for control was first experimented with over the Easter period in 1990 using three track sections and radio equipment which was hired. The experiment proved satisfactory with two train running, and although there were ideas for introducing automatic section signalling, these were dropped and the present system of control by radio developed. Radios were purchased and the full system brought into operation in 1991. The sets can be tuned to either the railway frequency or a frequency in general zoo use. There were some early operating problems while the system was settling down, and one member of staff from the catering department was trying to reach somebody and was told to use the railway frequency but declined on the grounds that 'it sounded like Heathrow Airport'!

There are now six track sections or blocks and when more than one train is required the line is controlled by a system of section occupation and separation. At intervals around the track circuit will be seen coloured boards mounted on posts and displaying a letter and a number. The red boards have the letter 'H' followed by a number in white, the yellow boards have the letter 'R' followed by a number in black. In each case the board has a border the same colour as the letter/number. These boards are section markers, 'H' stands for halt and 'R' for request. The colours were chosen to correlate to traditional signal colouring - yellow for 'distant' and red for 'home'. The total circuit is divided into six sections, each starting at a red 'H' board, a short distance before the start of a section is a yellow 'R' board. As a train comes up to an 'R' marker the crew radios the controller for permission to enter the next section. If permission is denied the train must stop at the next 'H' marker and is held at that position until given permission to proceed. On passing an 'H' marker, as soon as the last carriage has passed the marker board the crew call the controller to report they have entered the section. The controller keeps track of the progress of trains on the line on a board in the signal box which has an outline of the track diagram and hooks for each 'H' marker. There are red plastic tags for each locomotive which are moved around the board as calls are made and permissions to proceed are granted. The controller maintains a clear separation of one section between trains with the single exception that a train may be allowed into section 5 and then held at 'H6' (just before the level crossing at Central Avenue) while there is a train still in the station. The train will remain held at 'H6' until the station train has cleared the climb out of the cutting and across the road into section 2 in case any problem occurs on the rising gradient.

These control systems have proved to be completely safe, although procedures are periodically reviewed and new operating procedures issued from time to time.

All locomotives operate with two on the footplate, one of which must be a qualified driver. There is no necessity for a fireman in the conventional sense, but this allows the driver to give complete attention to the animals in the paddocks and provides a safety factor in the unlikely event of anything happening to the driver.

Avoiding animals in the paddocks is not a problem, the drivers get used to the way the different species will react and the animals normally move clear of the train. Generally, the animals are used to the passing trains, sometimes they will stand on the line or get between the railway and fence on the section which skirts the onager paddock and only move away when they are ready to do so. On occasion, however, they can run off across the grass, reacting as if they have never seen a train before in their lives! The most difficult time comes at the beginning of the year when the baby deer have been born. The mothers leave their offspring in a safe place and the youngsters' instinct makes them stay in that place, regardless of anything, until their mother returns. Unfortunately, the 'safe place' chosen by the mothers can be right between the rails. Fortunately there has been no known instance of an animal's death due to the railway. Certainly, the drivers find that every trip is different, short as the line is. On one trip with the diesel, the author had a considerable surprise when it seemed as if two large pieces of ballast suddenly rose up in the air about fifty feet in front of the locomotive - two little owls (wild, not zoo birds) had been on the trackbed and were completely camouflaged until they flew out of the way!

A steam train will normally haul five coaches, the diesel no more than four coaches on a train. This means most trains will be carrying around 120 passengers. On special occasions goods trains have also been run as demonstration trains to add interest for enthusiasts, thus three trains have been on the circuit at once, the theoretical maximum while maintaining a one section separation between trains.

The normal speed through the paddocks is 8 mph and the trip takes about 15 minutes. However, if the rails are damp and/or animals prefer not to move off the line it can take longer and in peak season the trip can be quicker.

Working the Locomotives

Since the first train of the day is not run until after midday there is no need for staff to arrive in the early hours to light up the steam locomotives. The normal starting time for staff in the morning is 9.00 am and the fire will be lit in the normal way for the locomotive/s to be used that day. Normally, there will only be one locomotive in steam, but two will be prepared for very busy times such as Bank Holidays. Once the fire has been built up satisfactorily, it requires only fairly minimal attention throughout the day to maintain an even fire, with periodic addition of coal and occasional raking as required. The fireman naturally keeps a watch on the boiler pressure and maintains the water level in the boiler, operating the injectors when needed. The steam locomotives use about two buckets of coal for each circuit, *Superior* is the most economical, *Chevallier* has the highest coal consumption. An engine can usually complete three round trips with a full tank of water. The tanks can be replenished in the station from the standpipe between the tracks at Whipsnade Central and filling is quite fast since these taps are connected to a large water main. Operating at Christmas time can however present a problem since in cold weather the stand pipe supply easily freezes up. If this happens, a hose is connected to the fire hydrant in the road behind the signal box and trails across the grass, over the platform fence, through the carriages stored in the loop and up to the locomotive - despite the Heath Robinson sound of these arrangements it all works perfectly well! When there are more than four coaches on the train, however, the locomotive is too far up the platform to reach the taps and the water tower in the yard has to be used. The locomotive is not uncoupled and moved up light engine, a train departs as normal and stops in the yard to refill. Passengers do not seem to mind the hold up while this is done, in fact, they seem to like it and consider the exercise all part of the experience of a trip behind a steam engine!

Towards the end of the day the locomotive crew let the fire gradually run down, usually relying on raking the fire over on the last trip to maintain it. When the last train has arrived at Whipsnade Central the coaches are uncoupled from the locomotive and the vacuum pipe disconnected. Lengths of timber are placed across the rails to prevent any possibility of the coaches rolling out of the station, the locomotive runs up to the yard light engine and stops by the coal heap. Coal is loaded by filling buckets which are manhandled onto the footplate and tipped into the bunkers, for *Superior* this will be twenty buckets plus two for lighting up next day. The engine is then moved forward and back over the points into one of the shed roads where the fire will be dropped and ash raked out. The engine will then be reversed into the shed for the night.

Staffing

With the very variable and seasonal nature of the traffic on the railway, it follows that the staff required is equally variable. The number of permanent staff has varied over the years. For the start of the 1994 season there was only one full-time employee, the Engineer and acting General Manager, Ian Gordon. Mr Gordon has remained in post, now as the manager, and is responsible for running the railway on a day to day basis. Decisions on major expenditure and strategy are made in conjunction with the park management, the railway manager reporting to the visitor operations manager who in turn reports to the chief executive.

Additional staff work on the railway either part-time or on a seasonal temporary basis. During the 1994 season, an Engineer worked at the railway for three days a week and the ex-Chief Engineer Richard Stanghan worked for two days a week. During the peak season there would be up to four staff working at Whipsnade Central. One person would always be in the booking office selling tickets and at least two others on the platform at all times. These staff would often be college students working during their summer holidays. On a Bank Holiday the numbers would rise to nine staff, four at the station, two pairs of locomotive crew plus two spare, and Mr Gordon controlling train traffic and coordinating operations generally. In addition, people who had volunteered under the community action scheme worked on track maintenance during the week, mainly replacing rotten sleepers. Occasionally some help is provided by volunteers who help out with maintenance and other tasks, although such help is on nothing approaching the scale of that enjoyed by Society run preserved railways.

The operating staff reduces as the season draws to a close and by late September the line was being operated by just two people, Mr Gordon and a seasonal worker. The method of operating then was for the booking office to be opened up a short time before the next train, or as soon as a queue began to form. After selling the tickets, the booking office would close and that person would move round to the platform to tear the tickets and allow passengers on to the train, the numbers being very low, perhaps a dozen or less. The gate to the platform would then be closed and while walking up the platform, the carriage doors secured. On reaching the diesel locomotive, the member of platform staff would join the Engineer and become the second footplate person for the trip. On reaching Central Avenue the train would be stopped and the seasonal worker would leave the cab and open the crossing gates. On arrival of the train, they would then unbolt the carriage doors and supervise the departure of the passengers from the platform. During the winter, track maintenance would be carried out by two people. In October 1994, a second member of staff working five days a week was allocated to the railway for a trial period to assist with catching up on arrears of maintenance.

Drivers are recruited from all walks of life, often doing driving turns at weekends, non-shift days or in their spare time, such as holidays. Currently there are drivers whose normal employment includes a coach driver, airline pilot, a London Transport manager, a barrister and an airline controller! A potential steam engine driver spends a season as a trainee fireman, then as a fireman who takes the controls for every other trip under the direction of the qualified driver. The speed with which a person qualifies is dependent on their aptitude and ability, it can be achieved very quickly, or never! Driving a diesel is somewhat more straightforward and can be performed under the supervision of a qualified driver by a seasonal worker who has been given appropriate instruction. There are three official levels of aptitude and responsibility on the locomotive side of operations: Passed Diesel Driver, Passed Fireman and Passed Steam Locomotive Driver. Each level is notified in writing by the railway manager when a person is deemed by the manager and other senior staff as having reached a suitable standard. It should be noted that the railway has women steam and diesel drivers and is not a male only preserve. Until the end of the 1994 season the drivers had always been paid, although the sum was small and really intended to allow for some measure of management control of 'staff' as opposed to volunteers. In reality nobody drove for the money and from the start of the 1995 season the payment system is being progressively phased out with the agreement of all the current drivers, thus converting them to a similar volunteer status as would apply on a preserved railway.

The staff have never been equipped with uniforms in the conventional railway sense. While she was the manageress, Mrs Haines brought in the use of green-polo neck sweaters to give a more consistent appearance to the staff who were in contact with the public. This idea was taken further by Frazer Crawley who introduced green sweatshirts displaying a yellow GWR logo. When the railway was taken over by the zoo, all staff were provided with plastic name badges and a form of uniform consisting of blue shirts, jumpers and pale blue trousers for platform staff, shed staff having their names displayed on their overalls. These innovations have now largely dropped out of use, staff dressing as they feel appropriate, although most of the platform staff will be seen wearing the official blue zoo T-shirt or sweatshirt with the 'Whipsnade Wild Animal Park' logo on the front and back. The locomotive crews' dress varies from the traditional engineman's garb through to a T-shirt and jeans.

The Volunteers who provide the train commentaries are not, strictly speaking, part of the railway operation but offer their services to the education department of the zoo. These people are not paid staff and usually come to the park for one day a week to help the zoo by undertaking various duties such as taking school children on guided tours, staffing information kiosks and the discovery centre, and their duties tend to be varied through the day. They will normally be wearing a red sweatshirt with 'Volunteer' in large white lettering on the front.

Accidents, Anecdotes & Questions

Although the trains travel at low speed, there are few turnouts and the single track is worked in one direction of travel only, it is also operating in a very different environment from most railways. There are large numbers of visitors to the zoo park in close proximity to the main station, the service is intensively operated with frequent trains carrying many hundreds of people every day during peak season, there are several road crossings on the level and the line runs through paddocks which house wild animals. It is particularly creditable to the staff and operating procedures, therefore, that the railway has an excellent safety record. No member of the public or railway staff has ever been killed or seriously injured. Moreover, no animal has knowingly been hurt or killed either. In conversation, a fireman did allude to 'a slight *contretemps* with a rhino' in earlier years. This was almost certainly a reference to the incident which resulted in *Superior* suffering some superficial damage to the casing of one of the cylinders - and 'ouch!' being daubed just above the torn metal work until repairs had been effected. This seems to have been a fairly even contest resulting in a 'no score draw'! The railway also seems to receive very few complaints. During the 1980s, there were a couple of mix-ups relating to school parties and there is a letter on file from a lady who complained of being covered in soot when she travelled in the open carriage. There was also one occasion when the railway re-imbursed a lady whose coat was burned by a rather large cinder from the locomotive funnel.

In twenty-five years of operation, the most serious accident on the railway occurred on 10th April, 1990 at the farm road crossing located between the yard and the first animal paddock. A five-coach train headed by *Chevallier* with the railway's Engineer, Ian Gordon, driving and the manager, Frazer Crawley, firing was approaching the crossing at about 2.35 pm and sounded the whistle about 30 yards before the road as normal. At the time, the zoo was receiving deliveries of earth spoil for landscaping work and driver Gordon saw one of the contractor's fully-laden, 35 tonne 8-wheel tipper lorries approaching the crossing from the right. The train brakes were applied and the whistle frantically sounded, but the driver of the lorry 'seemed completely oblivious and continued on his way' to quote the railway manager's report. At this point the line runs downhill and even at low speed (about 6 mph in this case) a fully loaded train weighing some 52 tons (including locomotive) and carrying around 70 people is unable to stop dead. Although all zoo staff know that the railway takes precedence at the crossing, the lorry driver could not have realised the railway crossing was there. In any event, he continued until the inevitable collision occurred. *Chevallier* hit the lorry on the nearside of the second steering axle and forced it some six feet sideways. With the forward speed of the lorry, the locomotive left the rails and slewed about three feet to one side across the rails and plunged downwards at an angle of some 30°, locked into the wrecked lorry just behind the cab. After getting over the shock, the driver of the engine recalls that getting the locomotive fire out at the angle *Chevallier* was now in, caused something of a headache. Despite the alarm caused to the passengers, there were no injuries and all were evacuated from the scene and returned to the station on foot, where they were given full refunds. The lorry driver and railway staff were also unhurt.

Despite the apparent situation, *Chevallier* had actually only suffered some scratches on the paintwork, a punctured vacuum hose and a bent lamp bracket. Unfortunately, the drain cocks were broken when the loco was lifted back onto the rails by the hired 50 tonne crane. The lorry, however, was more seriously damaged with a bent second axle and steering linkage. *Chevallier* was out of service for two days while repairs were carried out at a total cost of £12 plus one day's labour. No claim was made against Pleasurerail and the crane was paid for by the contractor's insurers. As a result of the accident, it was decided to erect large warning signs on the road approaches to the crossing, and relay the rail crossing in concrete. It was also decided to add gates which would be locked against road traffic while public train services were in operation, and against rail traffic at all other times - with Pleasurerail as the sole key holder. This accident was, and remains, unique in the history of the railway.

One would assume that a major worry for staff operating the railway would be a derailment in the animal paddocks. In fact, the only occurrence seems to have been the incident involving *Hector* in the tunnel, described earlier. There has been a derailment in the station area when a bogie on the last carriage of a train fell between rails which had gone out of gauge. The incident of the runaway carriage in the early years has already been described. A basic operating safety procedure in the yard is that the last turnout before the main line is always set for the headshunt, unless access is specifically needed to the main line. This prevents any runaway from the yard repeating the earlier unaccompanied journey through the animal paddocks. The potential value of this was nearly proven in more recent years. The manager, Mr Crawley, was hand shunting a flat wagon in the yard, which began to gain momentum. In his efforts to catch it, he caught his foot in the one of the points, resulting in his Wellington boot being pulled off. Gaining his feet once more, Mr Crawley set off in further chase of the wagon, wearing only one boot, and doubting he would catch it before it entered the headshunt with potentially embarrassing, if not destructive, results. He was, however, successful and caught up with it in time to pull on the handbrake, the incident is thus recalled with great hilarity. Slightly less amusing was the time when the driver of *Excelsior* was part-way round the circuit and called control on the radio to report that he could not close the regulator! With careful handling and use of the reverser the train completed a safe return to the station with the regulator still open. It transpired that three days earlier Mr Crawley had been working on the regulator and subsequent examination confirmed his fears - a spanner socket had been left inside the regulator housing and had worked its way into a position to jam the mechanism. *Excelsior* had also been involved in another incident which is recalled with some amusement. A newly qualified driver was taking his first 'solo' train and after crossing the road at the top of the slope had applied the brake. The rails were greasy and the locomotive and train started to slide. As he passed the yard the driver was seen to be waving energetically to Peter Haines, who realised this represented a plea for help, but could do nothing to catch the train, so he cheerfully waved back! He did, however, go round to the station to meet the driver, who was still shaking from the experience when he arrived. Apparently he was nearly into the rhino paddock before he had thought to release the brake sufficiently to stop the slide and regain some control over the engine! Mr Haines also recalls, with considerably less pleasure, the time when a coal delivery was made before the staff had arrived. With nobody around to tell him otherwise, the driver delivered 20 tons of coal, beside the track near the farm crossing! It took two days for the staff to get the coal back into the correct place in the yard. Following this, the gate staff were instructed never to allow a delivery driver into the park until a member of staff had arrived to supervise operations. Other incidents are covered elsewhere in the text.

Most railways have their store of questions asked by the public, one unique to this railway must be, 'Do we go through the tigers?' Grimy locomotive crews emerging from steam engine cabs have been asked, 'Is that makeup?' and 'Is that a steam train?' Booking office staff are inured to the regular, 'Does the train go to Kings Cross?' and are far too polite to offer the daft replies pinned to the (inside) wall as a response to, 'How long is the next train?' (about 150 feet), 'How much is the train?' (we will accept about £10,000), or 'I would like three adults please' (sorry sir, we only have animals in the zoo).

OVERALL LENGTH OF VEHICLE	WHEELBASE OR BOGIE CENTRES	MAXIMUM WIDTH TO CLEAR PLATFORM	OVERALL WIDTH OF VEHICLE
22' 0"	16' 0"	8' 0"	8' 0"
35' 0"	24' 0"	7' 4"	8' 0"

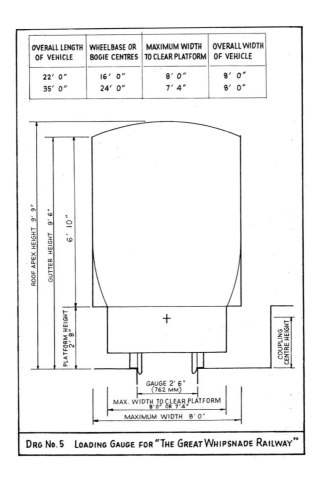

DRG No. 5 LOADING GAUGE FOR "THE GREAT WHIPSNADE RAILWAY"

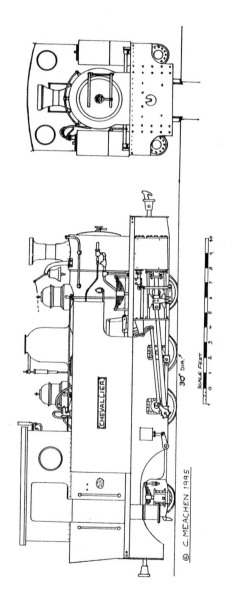

© Chris Meachen

Drawing prepared and reproduced by kind permission of Chris Meachen

Chevallier as in 1994.

Chapter Eight

Equipment

Steam Locomotives

No. 1 *Chevallier*

Type:	0-6-2 side tank
Builder:	Manning, Wardle & Co. Ltd
Works No.:	1877
Year Built:	1915
Weight:	28 tons in working order
Working Pressure:	160 lb. per square inch
Tractive Effort:	9792 lb. at 85 per cent boiler pressure

Chevallier was built for the Chattenden & Upnor Railway, a 2 ft 6 in. gauge line which was originally constructed in about 1885 to connect Upnor (opposite Chatham dockyard) with a Royal Navy depot at Lodge Hill. In 1904, it was taken over by the Admiralty, who continued to operate it. In all, 15 steam locomotives worked on this railway at various times, but only five remained at the end of World War II. During the following years the steam locomotives were replaced by diesels and all were scrapped except *Chevallier*. The Chattenden & Upnor Railway is now closed. In 1950, the engine was purchased by Bowater's and overhauled, although the appearance was not altered other than the addition of sliding windows to the cab sides and electric lights at each end, neither of which are any longer fitted to the locomotive. In 1968, the locomotive went into Kemsley works for a complete overhaul and was completely dismantled. The axles, complete with wheel centres, were sent away for new tyres to be fitted and the boiler, tanks and cab removed. The decision was then made not to proceed with the work and the wheels and new tyres (not fitted) were returned. The locomotive was put up for sale as effectively a set of parts for the new owner to sort out the reassembly! In October 1968, the engine was purchased by Mr W. McAlpine and delivered to his depot in Hayes, Middlesex as 'four lorry loads of bits'. By the following year, the locomotive had been reassembled and was in steam at Sandown Park after which it was taken to Mr McAlpine's stud farm at Henley-on-Thames, later to be joined by *Conqueror* and *Superior*. In 1970, the engine was taken to Whipsnade for the new railway and worked the first passenger train on 26th August, 1970. *Chevallier* was, and has since remained, under the private ownership of Sir William McAlpine and was never transferred to Pleasurerail Ltd. The agreement with Whipsnade requires basically that the engine should be kept in good working order.

A report prepared by Hunslet's in 1971 described the overall appearance of the locomotive as 'good' and the first manager of the Whipsnade Railway described *Chevallier* as 'a beautiful engine'. There does seem to have been some doubt about the state of the tubes, *Chevallier* being known as a fairly shy steamer, and the young Martin Johnson recalls that he often fell for the job of expanding the ferrules in the firebox since he was the only one slim enough to get through the firebox door, on at least one occasion doing this while the boiler was still hot. At some point in 1974, and definitely by June of that year, the boiler problems had reached the point where it was decided to strip the engine down, the intention being to do some other general work at the same time. It is believed that by now there was distortion in the firebox tubeplate, possibly caused by the loss of staying effect of the tubes, and the valve gear was also stripped, probably to correct general wear and tear. This work did not progress however and the locomotive was still not re-assembled by the end of 1979. It seems that the boiler was back on the frames by the begining of 1980, although the cab and tanks were not fitted to the engine. The boiler overhaul had been done by Maskells, but the re-assembly work had been further delayed by a break-in at the Whipsnade shed in early 1979 when the injectors and bronze bearings for *Chevallier* were stolen, together with the injectors and water valves from *Superior* and various pipes and fittings belonging to *Sezela* (a Knebworth engine also owned by Pleasurerail). The locomotive was finally reassembled and on Saturday 6th November, 1982, Mr W. McAlpine, accompanied by comedian Eric Morcombe, were on the footplate for a re-inauguration ceremony. *Chevallier* was put into service at Easter 1985, but immediately taken back out again, because she was damaging the track. Although there was nothing mechanically wrong with *Chevallier* the locomotive was used very little, if at all, after 1985 until Mr Crawley, the General Manager, decided to reinstate her to service in March 1990. The main reasons for not using *Chevallier* were the absence of vacuum brakes and the size of the locomotive. Since 1990 the engine has seen regular service and not required any significant work.

This is a large engine and really too big for the line, being somewhat tight for the curves, although that situation may ease when some of the planned track improvements have been completed. The engine uses a lot of coal compared to the other locomotives; on the other hand she is a powerful machine, capable of hauling six coaches packed with passengers at busy periods when a second locomotive is not in steam. At the beginning of the 1995 season it is intended to continue to use *Chevallier*, although she is really in need of a considerable amount of general attention and renovation to bring her up to peak condition. The side tanks stop short of the smokebox and on the top of the boiler are two sandboxes in addition to the dome, and a bell which is mounted on brackets secured to the top of the smokebox. Overall, this gives the locomotive a somewhat continental appearance. The aforementioned bell seems to have always been present on the locomotive at Whipsnade, but was not fitted when the engine was photographed at Ridham in June 1957. The locomotive is painted green, described in a Pleasurerail paint listing as 'Brunswick green' with smokebox, tank tops, cab roof and outlines of panels being black. Lining between the black and green is picked out in white. A brief note on the name may be in order since there are clearly two alternative pronunciations. Although the word 'Chevallier' is of French origin, as far as the owner of the locomotive, Sir William McAlpine, is concerned it should be pronounced as it is written in English with no accent at the end - so the name ends with an 'R' and not an 'A'. Since he has owned the engine for over 25 years, and this is the form always used by the Whipsnade railway, this seems to establish the correct pronunciation if only by custom and practice!

No. 2 *Excelsior*

Type:	0-4-2 saddle tank
Builder:	Kerr, Stuart & Co. Ltd
Works No.:	1049
Year Built:	1908
Weight:	14½ tons in working order
Working Pressure:	160 lb. per square inch
Tractive Effort:	5508 lb. at 85 per cent boiler pressure

Excelsior was one of three similar locomotives built new for the opening of the Bowater's Railway. They were known as 'Brazil' class locomotives by the builders, the other two were built at slightly earlier dates and called *Leader* (1906) and *Premier* (1904). On delivery, *Excelsior* cost £620 and was painted grey and had a steel firebox and tubes. The 'Brazil' class locomotives had 'balloon' smoke stacks at Bowater's to arrest sparks in the potentially combustible environment of a paper manufacturing plant and were designed to work round curves of as little as 40 ft radius. In 1968, *Excelsior* was withdrawn in order to become a source of spares for the other similar locomotives. This did not happen, however, and the engine was sold in October that year to Mr J.B. Latham, following a visit to Bowater's with William McAlpine, which had also resulted in the purchase of *Chevallier* by Mr McAlpine. *Excelsior* was delivered to Mr Latham in January 1969 and, following repairs, steam was raised for the first time under his ownership on 25th October, 1970. It has been recorded in other publications that *Excelsior* was purchased by Pleasurerail in 1971 and later that year was put into working order and taken to Whipsnade. This does not, in fact, seem to be quite correct. A privately prepared, and unpublished, book by Bernard Latham shows that *Excelsior* left his property on 15th December, 1970. This date is confirmed by the records at Whipsnade, which show that as early as November 1970, Hunslet (Holdings) Ltd had been contacted regarding drawings for 'Brazil' class locomotives and they replied on 1st December, 1970 with a suitable quotation for general arrangement and detail drawings. The fact that drawings were requested only a few weeks before the locomotive arrived confirms that negotiations for the sale of the engine were already under way, if not complete, by this time. A report simply dated as 1970 in the railway's files reported that the cab and tank were in good condition, but the locomotive was in need of a new smokebox door and the boiler fittings needed to be repaired and overhauled. The locomotive was also in need of new tyres, axle box brasses and attention to the brakes. On 31st December, 1970 an order to Hunslet's was confirmed for the fitting of new tyres.

On arrival at Whipsnade although the locomotive could be, and was, used it was in a very poor condition. The frames were in such a state that the chassis was literally moving under the engine and the valves and motion were considered to be worn out. Some work was done to the engine on site at

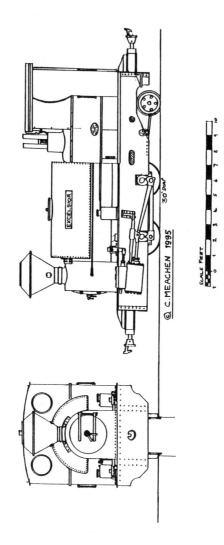

EXCELSIOR

© C. MEACHEN 1995

30" DIA

SCALE FEET

Excelsior as working at Bowaters' prior to arrival at Whipsnade.

Drawing prepared and reproduced by kind permission of Chris Meachen

Whipsnade, the railway files include two invoices in July 1971 from Hunslet for work done, 52 hours labour on 29th March, 1971 (presumably the start date of the work!) and 19 hours on 4th May, 1971. In July 1971 the manager, Trevor Barber, was offered a 3 ft gauge Kerr, Stuart 'Brazil' class locomotive (No. 3024) which had worked at the British Aluminium Works, Fort William, Scotland. The engine had no boiler, firebox, smokebox or boiler fittings and offers of over £150 were being sought. A deal was agreed and by 24th January, 1972 the remains of what was now referred to as 'No. 1', excluding the cab and bunkers, had been delivered from Mr & Mrs Curl of the Hampshire Narrow Gauge Railway Society. Mr Barber was not interested in the cab and bunkers, it was the moving parts which were required for a major rebuild of *Excelsior*. One source believes the work was done during the winter of 1972/73, however another is very sure that it was done in two stages, on balance this seems probable and is the basis for the following description. It has been said that *Excelsior* is now assembled onto the frames of a donor locomotive - this is not so. During the winter of 1971/72 *Excelsior* was totally stripped down and the existing chassis was re-riveted and bolted, finally being welded up into a firm structure again. The parts used from the donor locomotive included the cylinder blocks, eccentrics and entire valve gear from the 3 ft gauge engine - all re-assembled onto the repaired original frames. The original coupling and connecting rods seem to have been retained, as were the existing brasses on the axleboxes which were shimmed and repaired. A hydraulic test was done on the boiler and the locomotive was re-assembled and returned to service for the 1972 season. The next stage took place in the spring/summer of 1973. The engine was stripped again and the boiler re-tubed, this being a particular problem since the firebox tubeplate holes (being copper) were badly oversize, and some were oval! Other work included fitting new brasses to the coupling and connecting rods, fitting a grease lubricator to the eccentrics and the addition of an extended bunker to the rear of the cab. The locomotive was re-assembled and given a new paint finish ready for the time of the visit by Princess Margaret in August 1973. At Bowater's, *Excelsior* ran without a cab back sheet for part, if not all, of the time. At Whipsnade, she always seems to have operated with the cab open above waist level. What is different, however, is the additional coal bunker which curves outwards from the buffer beam up to waist level which, as noted, was added in 1973.

Excelsior was again out of use during 1974, the weak firebox had led to bulging of the tubeplate and the boiler was sent away for the fitting of a new steel firebox. The locomotive was back in service for 1975 and has continued to work reliably. When Peter Haines arrived to work on the railway in January 1980, *Excelsior* was stripped down for the annual boiler test and had no significant ailments. Within a month, the engine was back in one piece and used consistently again thereafter, the only work of any note being the provision of a new smokebox and smokebox door in about 1980. In 1985 the injectors, clacks and whistle were refurbished. During these middle years of the railway, prior to the fitting of vacuum brakes, *Excelsior* had only a hand brake, no steam brake being fitted. Mr Haines recalls that on one occasion the thread on the screw brake stripped and he continued to operate the train using the

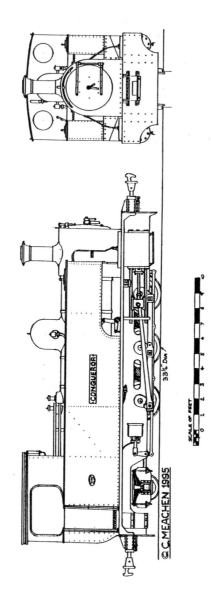

Conqueror as in 1994.

Drawing prepared and reproduced by kind permission of Chris Meachen

reverser lever to bring it to a stop when required. When, on occasion, the train was operated with only one person on the footplate, this also meant that when stopping to open the gates at the Central Avenue crossing or in the station, the driver had to smartly hop off the footplate and apply the carriage hand brakes to prevent the train moving back down the steep slope into Round Close backwards!

By the end of 1990, it is evident that the tubes were in need of work and a quotation was obtained to replace them all together, with the consequent cleaning up of the firebox and smokebox tubeplates. No work was done immediately, but for the 1994 season, *Excelsior* was withdrawn from service for the boiler to be re-tubed. The locomotive should return to service during the 1995 season, still with her original boiler. *Excelsior* can haul a full five-coach train but is considered a little light for the work. On the other hand, it has proved to be a generally reliable locomotive which has seen the railway through a large part of its life, by maintaining services while other locomotives were not available.

On arrival at Whipsnade *Excelsior* was painted green with the smokebox, chimney, cab roof and outlines of panels being black. Lining between the black and green was picked out in yellow, the overall effect being very much a match for *Chevallier*. At this time, the locomotive was already fitted with a straight chimney, replacing the 'balloon' stack fitted at Bowater's. On completing the 1973 rebuild, the locomotive was repainted and the colour scheme changed to one apparently intended to resemble the London, Brighton and South Coast Railway. The locomotive remained in this light brown scheme while in service until the start of the boiler work in 1994, the actual colour of the cab and saddle tank is 'saddle chestnut gloss' (BS No. 06C39) according to a Pleasurerail paint listing, with smokebox, cab roof and outlines of panels being black. Lining between the black and brown is picked out in white. On completion of the re-tubing work late in 1994, it was decided that for her return to service in 1995 *Excelsior* would be repainted. By Easter 1995 the locomotive had been further stripped down for the boiler inspection, which was successfully passed, and when re-assembled will be finished in a new scheme of Oxford Blue.

No. 3 *Conqueror*

Type:	0-6-2 side tank
Builder:	W.G. Bagnall Ltd
Works No.:	2192
Year Built:	1922
Weight:	28 tons in working order
Working Pressure:	160 lb. per square inch
Tractive Effort:	12,442 lb. at 85 per cent boiler pressure

Conqueror was also built for the Bowater's line and was larger than the previous locomotives built for the railway, including *Superior*, which had been built two years earlier with the same wheel arrangement. The side tanks extend forward to the smokebox and the sand boxes are not visible, being located between the frames. On Sunday 1st February, 1953, *Conqueror* had the misfortune to fall upside down into several feet of water, when a dock side collapsed as a result of an abnormally high tide. When the water level reduced, the locomotive was recovered, overhauled and returned to work.

Conqueror was still working when the Bowater's line closed and, being too large for the preservation scheme, various possibilities were being considered about the engine's future. In early 1970, the locomotive was purchased, with *Superior*, in preparation for equipping the new Whipsnade railway and was taken by Mr W. McAlpine to his private railway at Henley-on-Thames. Later that year it was moved to Whipsnade under the ownership of Pleasurerail Ltd.

Conqueror did not work at Whipsnade during 1970, indeed, in March 1970 a letter from Bowater's confirmed that the locomotive 'definitely needs re-tubing'. Quotations for the work, together with the construction of a new smokebox, were obtained and an order for the work was confirmed by Mr Barber on 5th January, 1971. A visit was made to Whipsnade by Hunslet's on 8th April, 1971 and their report described *Conqueror* as looking good overall, the boiler having been re-tubed and hydrostatically tested on 17th December, 1971. They felt that some further work was required including: reprofiling the tyres, the handbrake screw was worn, the sidebars and crossheads needed lining up, adjustment and re-packing of pistons and valves and the smokebox door required resetting to the ring. The locomotive was ready for work at Whipsnade in the 1971 season and was described by Mr Barber as 'a beautiful, docile engine' and it was this locomotive which was used for the Royal train in 1973. On the other hand, the running gear was considered a bit rough by some staff and this earned her the nickname of 'Clonqueror'! The engine does not seem to have required much work after coming into service. On one occasion repairs were required to the valve gear following a failure in service, the stranded engine and train having to be rescued by *Victor*. On another occasion a main spring broke while the locomotive was in steam and was immediately replaced, diesel haulage only having to take over for a few trains while the work was being carried out.

By 1977, the locomotive was out of use, requiring work on the boiler. Five new tubes were fitted in 1978 and, after passing a pressure test, was back in traffic for the 1978 season. Although the locomotive had been working during the 1979 season, further attention was required to the boiler and it is thought that the engine saw little, if any, service during 1980, but was in operation for 1981. *Conqueror* had a steam brake and was in fairly good condition, but was not very popular with the staff at this time for use on the line. The cab would tend to become very smoky and in summer could become uncomfortably hot. It seems that some drivers were known to have driven the engine while actually sitting on the roof, their feet controlling the very long regulator through the roof hatch - and this in the days of one-person operating! The steam brake was very powerful and the story has been told that when the rails were greasy it was not unheard of for the brake to be applied immediately after the level crossing and for the locomotive and train to then literally slide with locked wheels round past the yard right down into the rhino paddock. The locomotive took a very long time to raise steam, in excess of four hours, and this was a significant problem for a railway such as Whipsnade where staff would not normally arrive for work in the very early hours of the day and the locomotives are only required to work trains in the afternoons. In addition, *Conqueror* was very heavy on coal consumption, using about twice as much as *Excelsior*. As a result, the railway simply stopped using *Conqueror* at the end of the 1983 season and the locomotive was left uncovered in the yard. It is only fair to add that the locomotive was well liked by staff during the 1970s, although they tend to acknowledge that she was really to large and powerful for the line.

There were periodic thoughts about bringing *Conqueror* back into use and a list of jobs required was drawn up on 19th June, 1985 which included: re-tube boiler, injector feed pipe to boiler furred up, new brake blocks, 'all moving parts worn', overhaul water gauge glasses, cab steam valves and clacks need re-seating, vacuum brake to be fitted, replace cab floorboards, check front tubeplate for excessive wastage and possible replacement, reprofile wheels, new wheel bearings, replace loose and missing nuts on frame, re-metal crossheads, work on connecting rod and coupling bearings and cure radial valve play. Quite a list for a locomotive which had been working only some eighteen months earlier! No work was done and *Conqueror* continued to slumber where it had been left.

By 1990, the new manager was again considering getting *Conqueror* back into use and contacted Dorothea Restorations Ltd. This company replied on 9th March, 1990 confirming that the locomotive had remained stored out of doors since their last visit in 1984 and that it had visibly deteriorated. The locomotive was complete but in need of a fairly extensive overhaul, the boiler was known to need retubing, the platework had suffered and the smokebox was perforated in a number of places. They recommended a phased approach to the necessary work, with initial dismantling to assess the degree of work required, followed by drawing up a schedule of repairs. The estimated budget required was in the order of £50,000 to £100,000. The matter seems to have rested again until the following year when a quotation was obtained from a different source for repairs to the boiler, smokebox and firebox, including re-tubing. Although the cost of this was much more modest, it still would not have dealt with the other renovation work. Once again, no work was done.

By 1994, it had become obvious to the railway management that the necessary resources to repair *Conqueror* were not going to be found and the decision was made to try and sell the locomotive. The advertisement appeared in September 1994 seeking offers and by the end of September a sale had been agreed. By the end of November the locomotive had been moved to the end of the old station. Although stored in the open, the motion had been lubricated periodically and *Conqueror* could be moved easily on her own wheels by the Fowler diesels. The actual date of departure from Whipsnade was Thursday 15th December, 1994. The road transporter (of front loading type) arrived a little after 10.00 am and after detaching the tractor unit a length of track was built up on supporting sleepers to link the siding with the transporter bed. A Bowater's bogie flat wagon was located in front of *Conqueror* and with *Hector* pushing the flat, the initial attempt to load *Conqueror* was made. This plan failed, the angle of the temporary track being to steep, and resulted in *Conqueror's* front buffer beam grounding on the rails, together with the leading bogie of the flat wagon being lifted clear of the rails completely because of the relative angles. On letting *Conqueror* back down onto the original track the Bowater's wagon inevitably derailed. The situation was reconsidered and after the wagon had been returned to the rails a JCB was called in to physically lift a section of track, with sleepers attached, out of the formation of the siding. This was then packed with additional sleepers and ballast, and a more substantial support for the link track to the transporter constructed. The next attempt was performed by using the combined pushing power of *Hector* and *Victor*, together with a winch cable on the deck of the transporter. By about 2.00 pm *Conqueror* was safely on the transporter. After a tea break for all concerned, *Conqueror* was secured onto the transporter, the temporary ramp dismantled and the transporter tractor hitched in place. *Conqueror* finally departed from Whipsnade in the gathering dusk at about 4.00 pm bound initially for a workshop in Surrey. The purchaser was Peter Rampton, co-owner of the Brecon Mountain Railway Company, although it appears likely that the locomotive will become an exhibit in a proposed narrow gauge railway museum rather than see a restoration to working condition.

At the Bowater's Railway, *Conqueror* was equipped with a spark arresting 'balloon' smoke stack and this remained on the locomotive when it started work at Whipsnade. The colour scheme at this time was green with black edging, but no lining between the green and black. The chimney and smokebox were black and the buffer beams and connecting rods were red. By the time of the Royal visit on 2nd August, 1973, there was now yellow lining between the green panels and black edging, and *Conqueror* had a straight, conventional style chimney, apparently fitted somewhat earlier. Shortly after this, in the winter of 1973/74, the livery changed again, this time to a very dark blue. This colour appears to be black in photographs, and a colour picture taken in 1974 seems to show the entire locomotive to be painted in this single colour, with a simple lining pattern on the tanks and cab sides consisting of a single red line with quartered corners. It is possible however that the smokebox, and possibly the edges of the tanks and cab outside the red lining are actually black. Pictures taken in the early 1980s show the same arrangement, although again, it is impossible to distinguish for certain any difference in the colour on each side of the lining. A Pleasurerail paint listing quotes the colour for the locomotive to be 'Oxford blue' and it is understood that the colour was intended to represent the blue of the Great Eastern Railway. Examination of the rather weather-beaten and dilapidated locomotive sitting in the yard confirmed the colour to have been a very dark blue, the smokebox and chimney being black. There was also evidence of the lining pattern, which had the appearance of being a reddish pink, although the effects of many years in the open may have distorted this colour. It also appeared that the outlines of the panels were black but, again, weathering had made this difficult to determine with certainty. A person who worked on the railway in the 1970s has told the author that there was indeed black edging, but the lining was cream. There does not seem to be any doubt therefore that the dark blue was edged with black, and the photographic evidence of red lining is confirmed by the faded traces on the engine after many years out of service.

Victor passes the catch point after leaving Whipsnade Central on 28th June, 1979.

Zoological Society of London

Victor in mid-1994 on the yard headshunt with a Broughton Moor flat wagon.   *Author*

An early 1995 season train hauled by a freshly painted *Hector* passes two Pere David's deer - 'Mount Whipsnade' in the background.   *Author*

Hector outside the shed in 1994, to the right of the picture is a diesel fuel tank mounted on a Broughton Moor flat wagon.   *Author*

The Ruston & Hornsby 48DL No. 10 known as *Mr Bill*, in front is the Broughton Moor van converted into a brake van.

Author

On arrival at Whipsnade in 1991 *Nutty* was complete but not in working order. This picture shows the locomotive being unloaded at the road crossing adjacent to the old station. Note that the lifting barrier arm is still in place to the right of the road.

Peter Denton

Coach No. 10 pictured in about 1974/75, at this time still fully glazed and available as an 'all weather' vehicle.   *Graeme Carr*

A rake of coaches pictured in 1975 on the north side of the platform in the original station. The original transparent corrugated roof panels are clearly visible with simple fascia boards to give a finished appearance. In this picture the first three coaches are painted with grey side panels, the next is light green, another grey and one with red.   *Nick Robey*

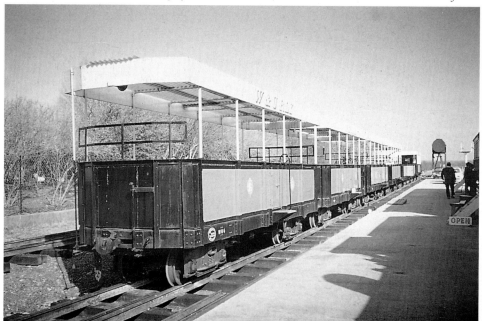

Top: The un-numbered open coach is the same as the closed conversions except for the absence of a roof and consequent supporting stanchions.   *Author*

Centre: Coach No. 10; originally fully glazed this coach is equipped for wheelchair access and has crosswise seating.   *Author*

Bottom: One of the standard coach conversions; pictured in 1994 this example is finished with red panels.   *Author*

The interior arrangement of the standard coach design showing the two sets of lengthwise seating and the loudspeakers mounted on the roof supports to convey the commentary.

Author

The interior arrangement of coach No. 10 showing the crosswise seating, remaining glazing at the far (brake) end only and the loudspeakers mounted on the roof supports.

Author

Top: An ex-Broughton Moor open wagon converted at Whipsnade into a ballast wagon with the addition of two hoppers let into the floor to allow the dropping of ballast between the rails. *Author*
Centre: An ex-Broughton Moor flat wagon, this example being fitted with raised ends. *Author*
Bottom: The ex-Broughton Moor powder van, converted at Whipsnade into a brake van, to the right is the front of *Mr Bill*. *Author*

This 1994 view shows the Ruston and three ex-Broughton Moor vehicles on the headshunt which was noticeably higher than the adjacent main line in the foreground, the 'H2' board signifies the start of Section 2 of the circuit. The headshunt was subsequently lifted in connection with levelling the site and construction of an access road. *Author*

The Smith & Rodley crane shown out of use behind the engine shed in 1994. To the left is an ex-Broughton Moor flat wagon with raised ends, to which three planks have been added to the sides in order to carry ballast. *Author*

No. 4 *Superior*

Type:	0-6-2 side tank
Builder:	Kerr, Stuart & Co. Ltd
Works No.:	4034
Year Built:	1920
Weight:	17½ tons in working order
Working Pressure:	160 lb. per square inch
Tractive Effort:	7555 lb. at 85 per cent boiler pressure

As with all the other steam locomotives, *Superior* was built for the Bowater's line. The three 'Brazil' class engines had been able to handle the work but, with the completion of Ridham Dock after the World War I, the traffic had grown to a point where another locomotive was required. The builder was the same as the earlier locomotives, but the new engine was to be a larger design, known as the 'Baretto' class, although it seems that only one other of this class was built, in 1919 for the 2 ft 6 in. gauge Dholpur-Bari Railway. In this connection, it is worth mentioning that the apparently similar locomotive *Joan*, now at the Welshpool & Llanfair Railway is not the same, being a 'Matary' class engine, modified with a larger 'Huxley' class boiler. The side tanks of *Superior* extend up to the smokebox and the locomotive appears not to have a dome. This is not, in fact, the case as there is a small flat-topped dome with the safety valves on top located on the top of the firebox. The locomotive was originally designed to be oil fired, but this appears to have been the cause of numerous problems and in 1921, the engine was converted to burn coal. At the same time, the steel firebox and boiler tubes were changed and a copper firebox and brass tubes fitted. There are two sandboxes on the top of the boiler and while at Bowater's the chimney varied between a 'balloon' spark arresting stack and a conventional chimney. At Whipsnade, the locomotive has also utilised both, but has carried a straight-sided chimney for some years now. *Superior* was also involved in an accident at Bowater's, the reasons not however being the same as *Conqueror*. In this case, the engine was derailed as a result of a side-on collision with some coal wagons and *Superior* ended up laying on its side. The locomotive was put back upright and after being cleaned up, apparently was back at work about three days later.

Superior was still in service when the Bowater's line closed in 1969 and in early 1970 was sold for use on the Whipsnade railway. As with *Conqueror*, *Superior* went to Mr W. McAlpine's private railway at Henley-on-Thames and later that year was moved to Whipsnade for the opening of the new line under the ownership of Pleasurerail Ltd. In a most instructive letter dated 24th March, 1970, a Mr R. McConchie of Bowater's wrote to Mr McAlpine 'The foreman who was in charge of our loco shop informs me that *Conqueror* definitely needs retubing, and that, although *Superior* was re-tubed three years ago, she has done a lot of running since and her boiler is in pretty poor shape.'

Superior does not seem to have worked any trains in the first years of the new railway, suffering from numerous problems. By the middle of 1972, however, thoughts were being turned to getting the locomotive running and on 5th October, 1972, Mr Barber wrote to Hunslet's informing them that he was

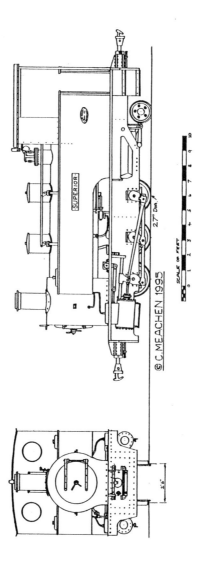

SCALE OR FEET

© C.MEACHEN 1995

27" DIA.

2'6"

SUPERIOR

Superior as in 1994.

Drawing prepared and reproduced by kind permission of Chris Meachen

considering bringing *Superior* into working order and asking for a quotation for new tyres '....bearing in mind we would hope to get the locomotive in motion by Easter 1973.' The subsequent quotation was received and a letter of acceptance sent on 7th November, 1972, the wheels to be sent on to Hunslet's for the work to be done 'in the next few weeks.' By now, the intention was to get all of the locomotives into operation for the Royal visit in August 1973 and this was achieved, although in the case of *Superior* she was still considered to be in a generally poor state. It has been said that the locomotive was only operating on a limited period of boiler insurance at this stage. The next work on the locomotive is not documented in the railway files, but Martin Johnson and Rod McLeod, who were introduced earlier, were closely involved in the next stage of the work done to the locomotive. Both the boiler and the motion required extensive attention and *Superior* was stripped down in the autumn of 1973 for a full assessment of what was required.

Extensive work was done to the motion and eccentrics, all brasses were adjusted and re-fitted, a bent piston rod was straightened and a broken piston was built up with weld. The tight economic conditions which the railway was operating under at the time even resulted in the re-use of some parts from the *Excelsior* re-build, and some valve gear parts from the British Aluminium hulk found themselves a new home on *Superior*! It was decided that the boiler could be used for the time being, although it seems the limited insurance ticket still applied, and on re-assembly the rear cab sheet was altered to the half height which remains now (as opposed to the earlier conventional full height cab back). This is one of the features which makes *Superior* popular with the footplate crew and the modification may be credited to Martin Johnson. Unfortunately he is unable to claim that the change was made with the future comfort of personnel in mind! What actually happened was that Martin was lifting the cab with the crane for re-fitting and it fell to the ground, destroying the rear sheet with a substantial crease across the top half. Necessity dictated the removal of the upper half with the spectacle plates, just allowing the lower half to be sheeted in. The chimney was replaced by using the original base and the 'balloon' stack from *Conqueror*. Martin had declared that *Superior* would be ready again by June 1974 and he met the target in the sense that her first steam trial on re-assembly was indeed in that month. Unfortunately no brake blocks were available, so the trial was conducted by taking *Superior* round the circuit accompanied by *Victor* acting as the braking mechanism. Overall this was a very low budget rebuild to provide a much needed locomotive and *Superior* was back in revenue service in August 1974 and certainly working passenger trains in 1975, she had also now been repainted red, full details follow below.

It had always been realised that proper attention was required to the boiler and by the end of 1979, *Superior* was definitely out of action again, being outside the shed with the back plate of the boiler buckled, no valid boiler certificate and a very sorry appearance. It is understood that she had ceased to be operable in about 1977. The situation was compounded by the theft in early 1979 of her injectors and water valves referred to above under details for *Chevallier*. The locomotive remained where she was until, in November 1982, she was dispatched to Steamtown, Carnforth with a lengthy list of work to be done. In

June 1983, Steamtown reported that the boiler had been lifted from the frames, the tubes and smokebox removed and new plates rolled. By December, they admitted there had been a period of inactivity, but by 10th January, 1984, were reporting considerable progress with the slide valves overhauled and reassembled, cylinders refitted to the frames, brake hangers welded and chassis platework renewed. The locomotive did not receive a complete new boiler. The front half of the boiler, the smokebox, firebox and stays were new, the rear half of the barrel and outer firebox were retained. *Superior* was finally returned to Whipsnade in July 1985, but the railway were far from happy, sending Steamtown a long list of faults they had found with the engine. Despite these problems, *Superior* was back at work on the railway by the beginning of August and saw out the season. Through the following winter the remaining problems were dealt with by a combination of Whipsnade staff and fitters coming down from Steamtown. By the start of the 1987 season she was available to be used, and although Steamtown wanted her sent to them for further work, the railway could not spare her away from the line during the Bank Holiday periods. The locomotive seems to have had vacuum braking equipment at this time, although in June 1987, the substitution of the existing vacuum cylinder for an 18 in. one under the offside footplating was still outstanding. Steamtown fitters were due to visit Whipsnade in July, apparently to deal with this, as well as adjusting the brake shoes on three of the newly fitted coaches. This period of the locomotive's history is commemorated by the wording 'Refurbished at Steamtown Carnforth May 1985' on the frame under the cab.

Superior has since then worked consistently, although she suffered a failure in May 1989, with bad leaks around the tubes in the firebox. The following August saw the replacement of 20 tubes and she was then back in service. A quotation for 12 tubes was obtained in July 1990 and on 22nd November, 1991, a quotation was supplied for 70 tubes to be fitted. The November 1992 boiler inspection observed that there were some 'slight leaks in furnace' which required attention, although the boiler was still passed for a maximum permitted pressure of 150 psi. The locomotive has also suffered a failure when the blast pipes collapsed, resulting in staff working through the night over a Bank Holiday to effect sufficient repairs to get her running again. These repairs were thought to be something of a 'bodge' but have held out since without further attention.

Superior is now considered the pride of the Whipsnade fleet, being the easiest to drive and most economical engine. Another plus point for locomotive crews is that with the back of the cab being open above the waist, the engine is much cooler on the footplate, especially on hot summer days - and when it is raining there are not many visitors in the park wishing to ride on the railway anyway!

On arrival at Whipsnade, *Superior* was painted in the same manner as *Conqueror*, being green overall with black edging but no lining between the green and black. The chimney was a spark arresting 'balloon' stack which was painted black, as was the smokebox, the buffer beams and connecting rods were bright red. In 1973 a straight chimney was fitted during the summer. Following the 1973/74 strip down and re-assembly the colour had changed to red overall with the chimney, smokebox, dome, coupler mountings, cab roof and outlines of panels being black. Lining between the black and cherry was picked out in yellow. The buffer beams and connecting rods were bright red. The frames were also painted red, though not the same colour as the tanks, the cab had the cut down back sheet and a 'balloon' chimney had been refitted. The red at this point had been intended to be Midland Railway crimson lake. In an effort to obtain a correct match the staff took a tiny tin of Humbrol 'Authentic Colour' (as used by modellers) to a paint supplier for an appropriate mix to be made. When the resulting paint was applied it was discovered that it was cellulose based, which caused the existing oil based paint to lift. Even worse, the colour looked nothing like the Midland shade they were seeking! In the end the colour applied was Crown Plus Two 'Royal Maroon'.

On arrival back from Steamtown, the full-height back to the cab had been reinstated, but this was quickly removed and the straight chimney had also returned to replace the balloon stack. The locomotive had obviously been fully re-painted, the colour scheme applied, which remains today, was essentially the same as the 1974 scheme, except that the tank tops and sand boxes are now black, as are the frames. There was also a small change to the panel/lining arrangement at the front corner of the tanks, which now have a rather unusual 'extra' vertical panel on the corner which does not have quartered corners to match the side and front panels of the tanks, the lining itself is now white. The red was however different!

The cherry colour was described by Whipsnade in the files in 1983 as LMS (Midland) Red 'as on Midland Compound 4-4-0 in York Museum'. There followed a complete chart, showing BS 4800 numbers and equivalent colours from the Dulux, Permoglaze and Magnet ranges. These are included here, since they may be of value, especially to modellers.

Part	BS 4800 No.	Dulux	Permoglaze	Magnet
Loco	04D45	Monarch	Cherry	
Edging	00E53	Black	Black	
Lining	10E49	Jonquil	Fiesta	
Cab Interior	none			Cream
Buffer Beams & Motion	04E53	Poppy	Flame	
Cab Roof, Running Boards & Boiler Bands	00E53	Black	Black	

Nutty

This Sentinel locomotive (see Chapter Five for full details) is owned by the Narrow Gauge Railway Museum Trust at Tywyn, Gwynedd. It was intended to put the locomotive on display to the public and restore it to working order, but it has remained in the yard in a dismantled condition.

Diesel Locomotives

Victor & Hector

Length:	19 ft 7½ in.
Width:	7 ft
Height:	10 ft 6 in. (top of cab)
Weight:	17 tons
Driving wheels:	2 ft 4 in.
Wheelbase:	7 ft

These two large 0-6-0 diesel locomotives are structurally and mechanically identical and their lives have largely been in each other's company. They were built by John Fowler & Co. of Leeds in 1951 with the works numbers 4160004 and 4160005 for the 'Groundnuts Scheme' and were structurally almost identical to the East African Railways '8000' class, apart from their gauge. The groundnuts project collapsed and the locomotives remained with the builders until 1954 when they were sold, together with a third similar machine (4160006), to the British Portland Cement Manufacturers Ltd at Lower Penarth Works, Glamorgan.

The engines are 4-cylinder McLaren M4 Mark 2 units developing 100 hp at 1100 rpm with the manufacture number 31315 (note - not the engine number). The cabs of these machines are quite large and they are driven in a standing position, in fact they have duplicated controls and can be driven from either side (although *Hector* has the vacuum brake control on the right of the cab only). In the centre of the cab are two large gear levers, one to select forward/neutral/reverse, the other being the gear selector for the four-speed gearbox. The locomotives have a heavy duty, dry plate clutch manually operated by foot pedals, although this is assisted by an air operated servo unit. The jackshaft drives the middle pair of wheels by a lengthy connecting rod and neither locomotive now has flanges on the centre wheels, although it would appear that they did when built, those on *Hector* having been removed in early 1987.

The 2 ft 6 in. gauge Blue Circle cement works railway system was abandoned in 1968, both locomotives being sold the following year, thus the locomotives became separated until re-united at Whipsnade. At this point, clarity will be best served by describing each separately.

No. 9 *Victor* - Works No. 4160005

At Penarth, the locomotive was that system's No. 5 and, being the most complete of the survivors, the engine having been overhauled not many years before closure, was purchased in 1969 by the Welshpool & Llanfair Railway. The story of its recovery and time with its new owners is well documented in the book *The Welshpool & Llanfair Light Railway* by Ralph Cartwright and R.T. Russell and in the *Llanfair Railway Journal*, the magazine of the W&L Society edited by Mr Cartwright. The W&L purchased not only the locomotive, but a large quantity of spare parts, including the engine from Penarth No. 3 (Fowler 4160006) and a set of wheels. The locomotive was transported to Llanfair on 9th August, 1969, and although it had been standing idle for some time and the outward appearance was not good, it was in good mechanical condition, and was soon running at its new home where it was subsequently named *Wynnstay* and became W&L No. 9. At Penarth, the locomotive had been green, the W&L repainted it in a darker shade of green, called Iona Green (BS6/074) with yellow lining.

The Welshpool & Llanfair has some quite severe gradients on its line and the railway found that the engine, manual clutch and gearbox made the locomotive rather inflexible and thus unsuited for passenger operation on their railway. The manager at Whipsnade, Trevor Barber, had previously seen the locomotives at Penarth and by early December 1971 had examined *Wynnstay* and been impressed by its condition and made an offer of £1,800 to purchase the locomotive for the Whipsnade railway. The offer was accepted on 31st January, 1972, and by the end of February a deposit had been paid and arrangements made for transport, the cost of £85 to be shared by the vendor and purchaser. On Saturday 18th March the locomotive left Llanfair and at 11.30 am the following morning was unloaded at Whipsnade with no undue problems. Trials were immediately held and overall Mr Barber was delighted with the new locomotive. The locomotive was delivered still with its W&L number plate, which it was agreed should stay with the locomotive at Whipsnade, explaining why the locomotive had, and retains, a number apparently out of sequence with the other locomotives, especially *Hector* which arrived some years later. The purchase also included the spare engine and about 3 tons of spare parts, but these items were not delivered with the locomotive. Separate arrangements were still being made later in the year, with the end of July being agreed as convenient. The name of *Victor* was decided upon very soon after the locomotive arrived and was chosen in honour of Victor Manton, the curator of Whipsnade Park.

Mechanically the locomotive has given very little trouble. In the winter of 1977 the head gaskets had blown and were replaced in time for the 1978 operating season. In 1983 Mr C.R. Morris reported that the locomotive had performed well for 10 years and no significant problems seem to have occurred since. If *Victor* has had a quiet life mechanically, it has certainly led a colourful life in terms of appearance! On arrival it was painted green overall, including the top of the bonnet, with a yellow line around the top of the engine covers. By about 1973/74, however it had been completely repainted and appeared with the frames, footplate, top of the bonnet and cab above waist level in black and the side panels of the engine cover, railing on the front of the footplate and cab to waist level in orange. The moulded strip around the top of the engine covers with a matching line around the cab was white and divided the black and orange. The cab roof and all connecting rods were a light colour, probably silver-grey, and the front buffer beam was painted with a 'V' arrangement of alternate black and white stripes (no picture has been seen of the rear to verify if this was the same). The W&L No. 9 plate was on the cab side and a *Victor* nameplate surmounted by a crest was secured to the top of the footplate about mid-way between the cab and front of the engine cover. A photograph taken in 1975 shows that the areas described above as orange had now become pink. At first it was assumed that the colour in the later slide may have changed with age, but a separate source has told the author that the locomotive was painted 'tangerine orange' and 'salmon pink' at different times, the intention being to replicate the appearance of a Canadian railway colour scheme. Further examination of the 1975 pictures show that a conventional *Victor* nameplate has been secured to the cab side beneath the number plate. It therefore seems that *Victor* has, indeed, carried two different and somewhat colourful schemes. Unfortunately, the railway does not have records of painting schemes applied to any of the locomotives or rolling stock for given periods, just occasional notes as to what standard colours should be used, buried amongst other papers! In 1980, when Peter Haines started at the railway, the colour scheme was definitely salmon pink and black and it remained so until about three years later when approval was given to repaint the locomotive in Brunswick green. This repaint gave *Victor* the same appearance as *Hector* has at present, being a mid-Brunswick green with black bonnet, except that yellow and black chevron stripes were applied to the buffer beams and the connecting rods were yellow.

Video film of the May 1992 *Steam Up* shows the cab to be a dark red colour, almost certainly a primer, since at the end of the 1992 season the colour scheme which remains today was applied. The present appearance of the locomotive is black overall with the following picked out in bright red: front and rear buffer beams, line around whole locomotive at cab waist height and above engine covers, stripe in the centre of the side of the footplate down its whole length, all connecting rods. In addition, the letters GWR appear in white with red shading on the engine side covers below the vent grilles. The nameplate remains in the same position on the cab side, but the number plate has gone and, confusingly, the number '8' is painted in white with red shading onto the cab side between the door and rear cab sheet. The presence of this number, together with the Works Plate 4160005 on the side of *Hector* led to the suspicion that the 'twins' had swapped identities at some point! Careful checking of the Whipsnade railway records and detective work with the current railway Engineer has led to the conclusion that the correct names are on the correct locomotives, it is the number on *Victor* and works plate on *Hector* which are wrong. The railway company files consider *Victor* to be No. 9 and there are traces of orange-coloured paint on the inside of the engine covers which confirm the locomotive's identity, since the other Fowler was acquired later than *Victor* and did not enter service until well after the 'foreign' paint scheme period. For the record, the engine number of the McLaren unit fitted to *Victor* is 43212.

Victor has not yet been fitted with vacuum brakes and cannot be used for passenger services, the locomotive is however used for works and maintenance trains. It is intended to fit vacuum equipment in order to provide a second diesel, and fifth locomotive, capable of working passenger trains.

No. 8 *Hector* - Works No. 4160004

At Penarth, this locomotive was their No. 4 and when the Welshpool & Llanfair people purchased No. 5 they anticipated being able to obtain a spare set of wheels when No. 4 was cut up. At the last moment, however, a member of the Welsh Highland Light Railway (1964) Ltd heard about the imminent demise of the locomotive and that company's Board immediately approached the owners, following which a purchase was agreed. The locomotive arrived at the Welsh Highland Company's depot at Kinnerley in Shropshire at about 11.00 am on Thursday 20th November, 1969. The Welsh Highland Light Railway (1964) company had been formed with the objective of restoring the Welsh Highland Railway in North Wales which had closed in 1937. In 1969 they did not, however, have access to the trackbed of the railway but were collecting equipment for future use at their depot. When the locomotive was purchased, it was felt that there would be no difficulty in re-gauging it to a nominal 2 ft and the locomotive was potentially more powerful than anything else they owned at that time, with the exception of the steam locomotive *Russell*. By 1975, the Welsh Highland company had still not obtained the trackbed of the railway they wished to restore, but did have a site known as Beddgelert siding in Portmadoc which, with a farm they also purchased, was to develop into a short length of operating 2 ft gauge railway. An agreement was arrived at with Pleasurerail whereby the Fowler and four ex-Bowater's wagons were exchanged for the steam locomotive *Pedemoura* in a straight swap. It should be remembered that Pleasurerail at that time operated a 2 ft gauge railway at Knebworth as well as the 2 ft 6 in. gauge line at Whipsnade. *Pedemoura* was at Knebworth and has no direct connection with Whipsnade. It may also be noted that the Bowater's wagons which did go to Whipsnade were not of the same type as the others already there, but of the older, timber-planked type, as opposed to the all-steel type at Whipsnade.

The Fowler was transported from Kinnerley to Whipsnade on 14th June, 1975 and this appears to have been a very taxing experience for the Welsh Highland people. After numerous problems loading the locomotive at their own depot, they departed in the early hours of the morning and arrived at Whipsnade at 7.30 am, to find nobody around to meet them. Eventually, their low-loader was manouvered into position beside the Zambezi locomotive and efforts were made to get the Fowler onto Whipsnade metals. Unfortunately, the Fowler then got stuck with the buffer beam on the rails. At this point, *Victor* was brought into action and, with much flying of sparks, dragged its sister locomotive back until two wheels were in mid-air. The low-loader was edged away to reduce the angle of the ramp and, after a final effort with some jacks, No. 4160004 had arrived at its new home! The Welsh Highland people then set off for Knebworth to collect *Pedemoura* and suffered more problems when they finally arrived at their own railway in Wales but that, as they say, is another story.

The locomotive had never actually been used by the Welsh Highland Railway and it is interesting to note that Trevor Barber had tried, as far back as 1971, to purchase it when he was manager at Whipsnade. Now it had finally arrived. However, nothing was done to get it back into working order until around

Christmas 1982 when Chris Morris, a part-time fitter at Whipsnade, started work on restoring the locomotive. On 7th June, 1983, in reply to an enquiry, Messrs Andrew Barclay replied noting with interest that Whipsnade were refurbishing Fowler 4160004 and experiencing problems with spares, and having to give the news that the supply of parts for McLaren diesels terminated in January 1982. In May 1983, an approach was made to Bedford Commercial Vehicle Division seeking help with refurbishing the engine. As a result, the Bedford Apprentice Training Division became involved and a year later the heads of the engine had been completed. On 7th June, 1984, Mrs Haines, manageress of the railway, wrote to Bedford's confirming their engineering was fine and that the railway was thinking of putting a plate on the completed locomotive to the effect 'Heads refurbished by Bedford Trucks', although this does not seem to have happened. Mr Morris continued to do, or supervise, the work on the locomotive and *Hector*, as this locomotive had now been named, was working again in 1984, but was not without its problems, since it had a reputation for leaving the track. It seems that the springs were not balanced and, to compound the problem, work was needed on the wheels. Indeed, a letter dated 22nd February, 1987, which Mrs Haines wrote to Mr G. Hinchcliffe includes the statement, 'When Mr Bill rode on her 2 years ago he said to get the wheels reprofiled' and goes on to say that the railway staff believed the track had deteriorated since *Hector* had returned to service. There was some dispute about this, since the track condition was known to be quite poor anyway, but in any event *Hector* was transported to Steamtown at Carnforth in Lancashire, possibly at the end of 1986, certainly by early 1987. The original objective had been to fit vacuum brake equipment, but while there the wheels were reprofiled and the flanges were turned off the centre pair of wheels. Once these problems were resolved, *Hector* seems to have become a reliable performer, the only other problem traced being that new head gaskets were needed in June 1992 and had to be supplied by a specialist. The gaskets were supplied and the locomotive returned to running order.

When *Hector* arrived at Whipsnade from the Welsh Highland it was painted maroon and pale green. When Whipsnade finished the renovation work and before the locomotive was put into service in 1984 it was repainted Brunswick green. The present colour scheme is that the whole cab plus engine side covers and front up to the moulded strip are green, as are the sides of the footplate. The footplate deck, front rail, cab roof and top of the bonnet above the moulding are black, the moulding round the bonnet at waist height is white. Both buffer beams and all of the connecting rods are red. The inside of the cab is painted green up to waist level and cream above, the gear levers, throttle controls and screw handbrake being red. Over the years the colours had faded somewhat and prior to the 1995 season it was decided to touch up the black on the bonnet - by the time the job was finished the entire engine had been re-painted, in the same colours, but it does mean *Hector* was now looking very dapper for the railway's anniversary year! Conventional nameplates for *Hector* are attached to the sides of the cab in front of the doors and on the cab sides behind the doors are the makers plates - for 4160005! The potential for confusion between the two locomotives has been mentioned above under *Victor*. It is believed that these plates were added simply to make the locomotive appear more attractive when it entered passenger service. For the record, the engine number of the power unit in *Hector* is 43221.

The nameplates for *Hector* bear more than a passing resemblance to those of *Victor*. They are, in fact, made from the same original patterns since it saved money to change the first two letters of the pattern which already existed rather than make a new one. Thus, *Hector* is not actually named after any person, although the owner of the foundry had a dog called 'Hector' which seemed to add a suitable symmetry to the decision born out of economic considerations!

Since *Hector* is fitted with vacuum brake equipment 'he' is able to work passenger trains out of high season and supplement steam hauled trains if required.

No. 10 *Mr Bill*

This is a small 0-4-0 diesel built by Ruston & Hornsby Ltd of Lincoln. It is a 'Size 48 DL' class locomotive, works number 221625, with a 3-speed gearbox and no clutch. The driver's seat faces to the right out of the open sided cab. The locomotive was built in a batch constructed between April 1943 and May 1944. The works number implies it would actually have been built in the earlier part of that period, sometime between April and December 1943. Another source, however, gives the year of manufacture as 1944. The works number also indicates that the engine is a Ruston 4-cylinder 'vertical' (i.e. straight, not V formation) rated at 48 hp at 1000 rpm.

This locomotive seems to have spent its entire working life at the Broughton Moor Military depot in Cumbria. It was supplied to Whipsnade by Messrs W Hocking & Co. Ltd for the sum of £2,500, the purchase order from Zoo Operations being made out on 29th June, 1992. Arrangements had been made for payment to be deferred until mid-September 1992, but delivery to the railway seems to have taken place either on supply of the purchase order or very soon after, in July 1992. The locomotive has remained unaltered since its purchase, still carrying the Broughton Moor Internal Number 'R7 No. 10', together with the Naval Number 'ND 6455' on the side of the cab. The bodywork is yellow and the frames are black. The locomotive also carries the legend 'Load limits - 5 trucks loaded, 8 trucks empty', again a reference to its military past.

A draft letter in the railway files indicates that the intention was officially to name the locomotive either 'Sir William' or 'Mr Bill', but the letter does not seem to have been typed up and sent, possibly because the question of financial sponsorship of the purchase was also to be raised and second thoughts prevailed! Nonetheless, the locomotive has become known to staff as 'Mr Bill' in the form of an affectionate nickname. It refers to Sir William McAlpine who has had such close connections with the railway and is known to many as 'Mr Bill'. Naming a locomotive in this way seems very appropriate when one recalls that *Nutty* acquired its name from the nickname of its driver, especially so when *Nutty* has spent many years also at Whipsnade.

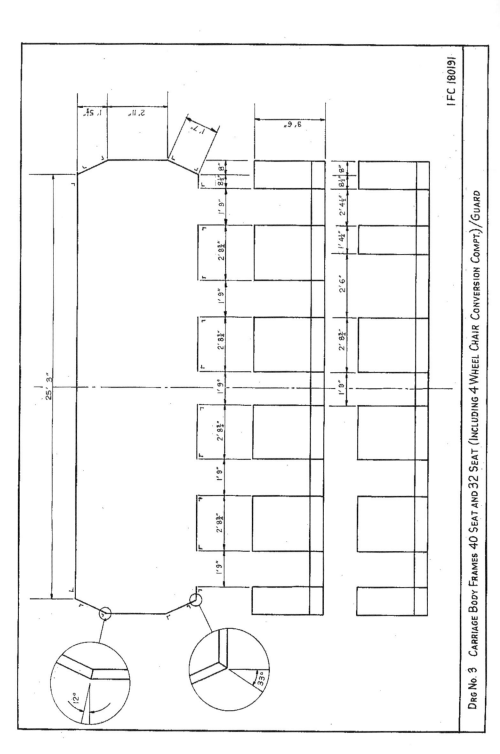

IFC 18019]

DRG No. 3   CARRIAGE BODY FRAMES 40 SEAT AND 32 SEAT (INCLUDING 4 WHEEL CHAIR CONVERSION COMPT.)/GUARD

Rolling Stock

The following list of carriages, wagons and other rolling stock represents every item of equipment present on the railway when surveyed in September 1994 and its use/condition at that time, together with other information as noted.

Passenger Carriages

The passenger carriages are all conversions based on the underframes, bogies and running gear of Pulp Paper wagons acquired from the Bowater's Railway in Kent. All of the frames were built by Butterly & Co. Ltd of Codnor Park, Nottingham, most still carrying the makers' plates; although some have become detached over the years, the outlines of where the plates were located still remain traceable. The conversions follow a basic pattern and all stock is generally compatible in appearance, however, not all the coaches are identical. The following description details the basic conversion, differences are detailed in the descriptions of each individual vehicle.

Basic Conversion

The underframes are of substantial steel construction and the floors are of metal plating, although some have become so poor in condition that wood planks have been placed on top of the original plating. The timber planks are mounted across the width of the frame, coaches so equipped are noted below. Square section, metal uprights are constructed to waist height, with a perimeter rail of the same section material to form the top of the sides. The sides and ends are sheeted-in to form a semi-open coach. Originally the sheeting was wood, although some vehicles have subsequently received plastic replacement panels, others retaining their wooden panels. Each end of the carriage also has a light metal frame to raise the effective height of the ends for additional passenger protection. There is a central door on each side of the body which opens outwards, with a corresponding metal step on the outside of the body to aid passengers' entry and exit to the coach. On each side, six metal tubular stanchions rise from the metal waist sections, at the top of which are 90° angle fittings and a horizontal tube across the top to connect each side (this tubular pipework was described as gas pipe and fittings by a member of the railway staff from the early years). When the carriages were first built, the roof consisted of corrugated transparent sheeting and boards were fitted around the sides and ends at the top of the tubular stanchions to give a finished appearance and hide the ends of the roof sheeting. The boards were secured to the tubular uprights by clips, which were not immune from becoming loose, with the result that the boards could actually slide down the uprights to obscure the passengers' view! These roofs were also very prone to leaking and it is certainly recalled that many a passenger received a soaking when water which had collected from overnight rain was suddenly discharged out of the roof and into the carriage!

These roofs remained for some years until the decision was made to replace them with new constructions of fibre glass. The plug was made to half length by Dunstable Sports Boats Ltd and the instruction to go ahead with the first lay-up was given in November 1982. The coaches were fitted with new roofs one at a time, two coaches being done each year, until all the stock had been converted.

The arrangement now is that a wooden beam runs lengthwise down the centre of the coach on top of the cross tubes and this supports the centre of the new style roof. The roof actually consists of two mouldings joined together and wraps downwards from the eave giving the appearance of a large lid on the coaches. Each carriage has seating arranged lengthwise along the coach so that passengers face outward for clear viewing of the animals. The seats are in the form of two back-to-back pairs with a gap in the centre corresponding to the door openings and are constructed with a light, square section metal frame with wood slats forming the seats and backs. Each carriage accommodates about 25 people and is equipped with two loudspeaker units suspended from the roof frames to relay the commentary provided during the circuit.

The underframes are all painted black, the waist framing and upright stanchions supporting the roofs are painted cream up to the roof edge, and the roofs are light grey. The additional frames above the waist rail at each end are painted black. The metal seat frames are black and the slats are either varnished or painted brown.

Not all of the coaches are equipped with vacuum brakes, five are fully fitted and the rest are piped only. Trains are always marshalled with the piped-only stock at the front, the braked vehicles being at the rear. Normally this means a train consists of the locomotive, then two piped coaches, then three fully vacuum braked coaches.

Individual Carriages

Details regarding livery, braking equipment, etcetera, represent the situation at the end of the 1994 operating season. The coach numbers are located on the inside of the ends of the roofs and relate to the numbers carried in 1994. Coach numbering does not seem to be very exact and these numbers vary from a list prepared a few years earlier, for instance, No. 10 was then clearly No. 6. No attempt has been made to trace each coach back through its individual history, since such an exercise seems both impossible and, frankly, pointless in view of their design!

No. 1   The passenger section of this carriage finishes short of the end of the coach, with a separate platform formed between the passenger accommodation and the actual end panel. This compartment has a vertical hand brake wheel and a seat for the person giving the commentary during the trip round the line, together with a microphone. The side accesses are open and protected by light chains hooked across the gaps. This vehicle would always be marshalled as the first carriage of a train. The body panels are painted green both on the outside and inside and the carriage has a wood floor. This vehicle is piped only and does not have vacuum brakes, braking equipment being the afore- mentioned screw brake only.

No. 2   Standard conversion with roof, the body panels are painted green both on the outside and inside. This carriage has full vacuum braking equipment.

No. 3   Standard conversion with roof, the body panels are painted green both on the outside and inside. This carriage has full vacuum braking equipment.

No. 4   Standard conversion with roof, the body panels are painted green both on the outside and inside. This carriage has full vacuum braking equipment.

No. 7   Standard conversion with roof, the body panels are painted a dark red on the outside and green on the inside and the carriage has a wood floor. This carriage has vacuum piping only, the brakes are applied by the side hand brake lever for parking.

No. 8   Standard conversion with roof, the body panels are painted a dark red on the outside and green on the inside. This carriage has full vacuum braking equipment.

No. 9   Standard conversion with roof, the body panels are painted a dark red on the outside and green on the inside and the carriage has a wood floor. This carriage has full vacuum braking equipment.

No. 10   There was a scheme some years ago to convert this vehicle into a railcar and some evidence of the preliminary work towards this remains under the floor of the frame. The idea was dropped and it became a coach as described below.
Although of similar outward appearance to the other carriages, this vehicle is actually somewhat different. It has an end compartment similar to No. 1 with the brake wheel, seat and microphone equipment, but the internal arrangements of the passenger section are completely different from the others. The vehicle has four internal compartments, each accessed by their own door, but with doors on one side only. The door for the compartment nearest the brake end is wider than the others to allow access for wheelchairs, sufficient room being available in the compartment for wheelchair users to sit facing the fitted seats. The compartments are divided by three sets of back-to-back seats arranged across the full width of the body in conventional style. The seats are constructed in the same manner as for the other vehicles. The floor of the carriage is wood, the planking arranged across the width of the vehicle. The uprights from the waist to support the roof are much more substantial square tubular sections than for the other carriages, being the same as the waist rails. At the bottom edge of the roof line, metal angle strips surround the carriage and support the tubular pieces which run crossways to support the roof, as in the standard conversions. The brake end has glazed windows, the other end is of similar construction but the windows are not glazed. Originally this vehicle also had full glazing all round, being intended as an all-weather coach from the beginning of the railway, but the other glazing was removed in 1990. The sides are therefore also open above the waist. The internal seating arrangement was altered to the present in order to provide a vehicle for disabled accessibility in the winter of 1990/91. The body panels are painted red both on the outside and inside. This vehicle is semi-fitted having vacuum operated brakes on the rear bogie only, the front bogie has screw operated brakes.

No No.   A standard conversion up to the waist rail but with no roof or consequent support stanchions. The body panels are painted green both on the outside and inside. This carriage has vacuum piping only, the brakes are applied by the side hand brake lever for parking.

A further conversion is in progress (September 1994). This will be a bogie carriage similar to No. 10 with conventional transverse seats, but with five internal compartments. Again, the doors are on one side only. The body panels are painted dark red.

Livery
The livery given above details the colours in 1994, but the coaches have not always been painted as they are at present. When the railway first opened, the side panels of the coaches appear to have been green with ornate lining out of four large panels on each side, together with the doors and small panels on each side of the doors. The side panels of the roofs bore the full title 'WHIPSNADE & UMFOLOZI RLY' written down their lengths. A slightly later photograph shows the roof side legend to have reduced to 'W & U RLY' in yellow, defined from the yellow background by black outlining shaded to give depth. The coach sides were clearly green with a black band at the waist top, the side panels were lined out in yellow and the railway's crest appeared on the coach sides as well.

Photographs taken in 1975 seem to show a transitional period with the roof panels as above but the sides of some coaches plain green, others plain grey with black ends and others still in a brownish red (this could be the current dark red, it is possible the colour quality of the transparency has suffered with age). By the early 1980s, at least one train of coaches had the grey sides with no lined panels or crests, the roof stanchions and roof panels were still yellow but without any lettering on the sides. All metalwork up to and including the waist rail was black. The yellow roof side panels would have finally disappeared when the design of the roofs was changed to the fibre glass 'envelope'.

A Pleasurerail paint listing has been found which quotes the various paint colours for coaches as follows:

BS 08 51   Gold Cup Gorse gloss, coaches
BS 12B25   Chive Thyme gloss, coaches sides
Magnet 521   Brilliant Green, coaches

Non-Passenger Rolling Stock

There is no goods traffic on the railway but a number of items of rolling stock are required for maintenance work and other special purposes. On special occasions, 'goods' trains have been worked around the full circuit as demonstration trains, along with passenger workings.

There are nine vehicles based on the same design of 4-wheel underframe which is 11 ft 1 in. long and 4 ft 4 in. wide. All the wagons have decks of wood planking fixed crosswise on the frames, they also have a long handbrake lever on each side, pivoting from a central position on the frame where it activates the brake on each wheel. The handle end of the lever is to the right when facing the vehicle, the handle being roughly level with the end of the frame, a ratchet frame hangs vertically from the vehicle frame to keep the brake in the position set. The wheels run in Timken bearings and there is a coil spring for each wheel. These vehicles all came from the Broughton Moor Military Railway and were acquired in 1992, as described earlier. They seem to have arrived at Whipsnade around the period June to August 1992 and fall into four types - two vans (understood to have been powder vans when in military service), one 2-plank wagon, two flat wagons and four flat wagons with raised ends. Only five of the wagons are actually owned by the Whipsnade railway, the four flat wagons with raised ends being privately owned. Their owner was unable to store them himself and Mr Crawley agreed to provide 'storage' at Whipsnade on the condition they were allowed to use them while at the park. Unfortunately, none carry numbers which clearly identify them so each is described below as an individual unit, the dimensions are only quoted once for simplicity but apply equally to the other similar items of stock. Towards the end of 1994, the position regarding the four wagons on the railway but not owned by it were under discussion, a probable sale by their owner to another railway seems likely with their consequent removal from the line, they were all still present at Easter 1995 however. All the wagons are painted in a similar manner with the woodwork being light grey, the frames, axleboxes and supporting metal for the bodies being black. Several are lettered 'GWR' in white:

4-wheel flat wagon with raised ends. This is basically a flat wagon with metal uprights at each end to which are fixed three wood planks with gaps between each. The total height from the bottom edge of the frame to the top of the upper plank is 3 ft 4 in.

4-wheel open wagon. The sides are formed by two planks supported by ironwork, the ends are formed from four planks, the top two being cut to a curved outline, thus forming ends which in the centre are higher than the sides. The height from the bottom edge of the frame to the centre of the top plank on the end is 2 ft 9½ in. This wagon has been converted into a ballast wagon by the addition of two hoppers under the floor which, when opened by turning the handwheel on one side, drop stone into the centre of the track. This vehicle has a hand brake lever on one side only.

4-wheel closed van. Marked No. 6 and 'Weight 6 tons'. This small van has a ridged roof with two sliding doors in the centre corresponding to the side doors. There are two doors on each side, each 2 ft 6 in. wide, opening outwards. The roof doors run on rollers which locate in channels mounted at the top edge of the sides just under the eaves of the roof, each slides back along the roof towards the ends when opened. The sides have eight planks, the ends a ninth to provide the additional height at the centre ridge. This van was converted at Whipsnade into a brake van and has a small window in the centre at one end, the other end is equipped with two metal steps and a handrail. The length is 11 ft 1 in. as for the wagons, but the body has an overall width of 4 ft 7½ in. and the height of the body to the top of the sliding roof door runners is 5 ft 4 in.

4-wheel flat wagon. This wagon carries a large cylindrical tank containing diesel fuel supported on a gantry made up from angle iron. The tank and gantry are painted green.

4-wheel flat truck. This wagon carries a square green tank marked 'Kero' in black on the end. The tank is supported clear of the bed of the wagon by four sleepers and contains kerosene (or paraffin).

4-wheel closed van. Marked No. 4 BV and 'Weight 6 tons'. As with the other small van, this is of the same construction with a ridged roof and sliding doors, and two doors on each side opening outwards. The construction of the body is the same as for the other van, except there are two metal steps and a handrail on both ends, and no window.

4-wheel flat wagon with raised ends. This is basically a flat wagon, with metal uprights at each end, to which are fixed three wood planks with gaps between each. At the time of survey this wagon was loaded with the tank, sheeting and other parts from the locomotive *Nutty*.

4-wheel flat wagon with raised ends. This is basically a flat wagon, with metal uprights at each end, to which are fixed three wood planks with gaps between each. Two planks of wood have been crudely attached to form rough sides to the wagon in order to contain a load of track ballast. The additional planks on the sides are unpainted.

4-wheel flat wagon with raised ends. This is basically a flat wagon, with metal uprights at each end, to which are fixed three wood planks with gaps between each. Three planks of wood have been crudely attached to form rough sides to the wagon in order to contain a load of track ballast and are unpainted.

The remaining three items of rolling stock in use are as follows:

Ex-Bowater's Bogie flat wagon. This is simply the Bowaters frame with a flat metal sheet floor, nonetheless it is a useful wagon which can carry large or heavy items.

Small 4-wheel unsprung skip wagon. This wagon has a 'V' body to allow a load to be tipped out on either side. The wagon frame and outside of the skip body are painted black, inside the body is now rust in colour! This wagon appears to be one of two which were purchased in 1971, an account from Alan M. Keef of Bampton, Oxford, dated 18th September, 1971 referring to two 2/3 yard tipping wagons delivered Whipsnade 17th September, 1971 as agreed at £25 each.

Small 4-wheel trolley. This wagon is of very crude construction with a metal floor. The curved spoke wheels run on inside bearings (no axle boxes) with no springing.

Miscellaneous Stock

Rail mounted crane. This is a standard gauge 5-ton capacity crane built in 1936 by Smith & Rodley of Leeds. The crane has a full cab built from vertical wood planking and has a number of windows, most still glazed. The roof is also of wood. A third rail is in place down the outside of the narrow gauge siding on the west side of the engine shed. The crane could be run from the north end of the siding where there is road access behind the shed, up to the other end in the yard proper, where the dual gauge rails pass over an inspection pit. The crane was present at the railway from the beginning and extensive use was made of it in the early days. It was still operating in the 1980s, but by the end of 1988 the travelling gear was not working properly and spares were hard to obtain, if not impossible. It steadily fell out of use and is no longer in working order. Being surplus to the railway's requirements it was advertised for sale in October 1994. The feelings of staff towards this crane seem to have been quite mixed. One person from the early days was quite saddened to hear it was no longer in use, but another thought it one of the most lethal pieces of equipment he had come across, recalling that the engine was started by removing the air cleaner and holding a lighted rag over the intake - the only time he had seen flames licking downwards as opposed to rising!

There are three further Butterly built ex-Bowater's bogie pulp wagon frames in the yard. None presently are mounted on bogies, although the bogies are also stored elsewhere in the yard. Two of these frames are stacked and available for conversion in the future, indeed, one has already had the body support uprights attached along with part of the waist railing. The third is used as a platform to support the storage of firewood and oil cans, although it could be 'rescued' if required in the future.

The railway used to own six further Bowater's wagon frames which were sold in November/December 1993. As part of the price obtained for *Conqueror*, four of these frames returned to Whipsnade in early 1995, providing a store of parts for the existing coaches and the potential for further conversions in the future.

There is also a chassis in the yard for a 4-wheel skip wagon, the body is not presently mounted on it but can be found laying in another part of the yard. The frame is sufficiently rust-covered to eliminate any trace of the colour, the separated body is also black, as for the complete wagon. This would appear to be the remains of the other skip wagon in use at Whipsnade from the time the line was built.

Past Stock

In a period of 25 years it is inevitable that equipment will be disposed of for various reasons. The following items have been identified as having, at some time, been on the railway:

Ruston & Hornsby 0-4-0 Diesel

This locomotive was built in 1961 with works No. 435403. It was one of three built to a flameproof design supplied by the makers to John Lysaght Ltd of Scunthorpe for use in their Nettleton Top iron ore mines. The engine was a four-cylinder Ruston '4 YEF' engine rated at 75 bhp at 1500 rpm, the gearbox being a Ruston patent four-speed, oil operated, constant mesh type with a low pressure, hydraulically operated cone clutch. Reversing gears were incorporated in the gearbox. Drive was by jackshaft to the coupled wheels. The locomotive was 13 ft 10½ in. long, the wheelbase 4 ft 0 in. and the weight in working order was 10 tons. The appearance was of a typically compact mine design. The locomotive was at Whipsnade from 1970 but was not considered a success. In fact, the staff at that time thought it had a mind of its own, with controls that did not appear to have the same function from one day to the next! In May 1971, in reply to an enquiry from Mr Barber, English Electric-AEI Traction Ltd supplied drawings 'which may be of assistance when you rebuild your LHU machine.' Nobody apparently mastered operating the locomotive and it was offered for sale. An enquiry was received from the Sittingbourne & Kemsley Railway in Kent and Mr Barber replied on 15th July, 1972 giving general details, including information that it had been temporarily modified to drive at one end, adding that the locomotive was in working order. The S&K responded on 1st October with an offer to purchase the locomotive, spares and ancillary air compressor for £100. The offer was accepted on 4th October, and on 18th October, 1972, the new owners wrote to confirm that the locomotive had arrived without incident on 'Friday evening'. The speed at which this deal was concluded may give some indication of the feelings of the Pleasurerail staff towards this machine! The new owners named the locomotive *Edward Lloyd*.

Motor Rail 0-4-0 48 hp Diesel
Built in 1935 originally to 3 ft gauge and worked for the London Brick Company. This locomotive was used for maintenance trains and remained in the yellow livery of its previous owners. An account for £200 from Alan M. Keef of Bampton, Oxford dated 23rd March, 1971, was supplied for Simplex locomotive No. 5060 regauged to 2 ft 6 in. and delivered to Whipsnade on 17th September, 1971. It seems to have fallen out of use by the end of 1976, possibly earlier, and was sold by the middle of June 1983 (see below).

A battery powered locomotive arrived at the railway in about 1974 and was subsequently used for works trains, although it was rather prone to derailments. The maker is not known although an ex-employee thought it may have been built by Lister. The driver sat sideways and it seems to have been painted green on arrival, but by 1977 is thought to have been blue in colour. It was charged up overnight and ran on its own batteries until they were exhausted, hopefully not out in the animal paddocks! In addition to the above mentioned Motor Rail locomotive, two other Motor Rail diesels seem to have appeared on the railway sometime after 1973, but virtually nothing is known about them. The battery locomotive, together with all three Motor Rail locomotives, seems to have been taken away from the railway in June 1983 after being sold to Alan Keef Ltd, the sale apparently having been agreed in the previous year.

Permanent Way

The survey of the railway carried out by Mr S.A. Pearson of the British Safety Council on 27th July, 1972, describes the permanent way of the new railway and refers to the main line as consisting of 30 ft lengths of 60 lb. per yard rail and the siding rails as heavier at 75/80 lb. per yard. The rails were described as being supported by sole plates and secured to wooden sleepers by three 5 in. spikes -

two inside and one outside. Four bolt fish plates were used throughout the system. The weight of rail is interesting but must be an error as the first manager of the railway has stated that the new line was all laid with newly purchased 75 lb. per yard flat bottom rails on wooden sleepers with granite ballast. The heavier weight of rail is confirmed by the present manager and Engineer and, since the original rails laid in 1970 are still in use and have not required replacement, this would seem to be correct. Unfortunately the situation is complicated by the 1986 Railway Inspectorate report by Mr Abbott (previously referred to) in which the rails were noted as having been laid in two stages, stage 1 of one mile being laid in 85 lb. per yard flat bottom rail, and stage 2 also of one mile in 65 lb. per yard flat bottom rail. Since, of course, the railway was indeed laid in two stages, this statement does seem convincing and may well reflect the true situation. The pointwork for the yard sidings was made up from standard gauge material which came from Kempton Hardwick power depot near Wilhampstead. The track had already been lifted and the parts were brought to Whipsnade and laid by volunteer enthusiasts. Whatever the exact weight of rail, the track is quite heavy for a narrow gauge railway. The sleepers are spaced about 20 inches apart and spot replacement is performed as required. If a rail became so worn as to require replacement the old length would simply be lifted out and a replacement put in its place. The track ballast is conventional granite stones. Overall, experience has shown that several of the curves were laid at too tight a radius, thus causing excessive wear to locomotive wheels. This seems surprising, considering that it was always planned that the locomotives on the railway would be quite large, six-coupled narrow gauge engines, although Tom Hill, who surveyed the line, points out that the layout was constrained by various unavoidable factors. The worst curve (almost a corner!) is in the yard around the 'H2' marker board and it is planned to ease this in the foreseeable future. All points are operated by weighted levers adjacent to the turnout.

Maintenance of the track is carried out between October and March while the line is closed to the public. Work on the track in the paddocks is done without any special arrangements being required concerning the animals and does not normally cause any problems for the maintenance gang. If an animal does become a nuisance the crew can just retreat to the cab of the locomotive. Inevitably, of course, there are stories which arise from the unusual, if not unique, operating environment. In the days of the original rhino paddock there was an instance when the maintenance workers had pulled out an old sleeper for a spot replacement, following which a rhino arrived on the scene and playfully pushed the sleeper back into place! In more recent years, Frazer Crawley was digging out a hole by hand in Round Close when a particularly cheeky swamp deer arrived unseen behind him and proceeded to attempt what should normally only be done with a female of its own species. The animal, however, came off somewhat worse as Mr Crawley was so startled by the hooves which unexpectedly appeared on his shoulders that he jerked bolt upright so suddenly that the swamp deer was bowled over to the ground backwards!

There are several things which make this railway unique, one being the civil engineering constructions known as ha-has. This term does not derive from the railway but is believed to date back to the time of large country houses with deer parks. To prevent deer from encroaching on the lawns around the house, they were fenced, but the fence was placed in the bottom of a ditch so as to disguise it from the house and give an apparently uninterrupted vista for the gentry.   At Whipsnade they each consist of a combined ditch and bridge and act in conjunction with adjacent fences. The purpose is to let the train pass between the different paddocks without the animals being able to do so. They work perfectly well, although some of the more athletic and adventurous animals jump fences occasionally and get into the wrong paddocks! They are not of identical design and a description of each is given in the detail of the route. It will be noted, however, that those up to Umfolozi Halt are of a much more complex design than the remainder. It may be thought that this is because they were designed and constructed at different times. However, the ha-ha at Umfolozi Halt, although of the same design as the original one at the entry to the rhino paddock which was built for the opening of the railway, was built when the line was extended and at the same time as the remainder. The author has been told that it is now considered that several of the bridges are over engineered and capable of supporting far higher loads than are ever likely to be required. Having said that, there have been occasions when double headed trains have been operated and the additional strength was probably just as well!

Bactrian Camel

Chapter Nine

The Animals

A ride on the railway offers the best view of a number of the animals in the park, mainly the Asian species. Even in the 'Passage Through Asia' where visitors can drive their own cars across Cut Throat paddock and Valley Meadow the road passes across different areas of the paddocks and, of course, many visitors do not drive their own cars inside the park.

During the summer, a commentary is given during the ride by zoo volunteers, based on a script supplied by the zoo education department. The 'Vols' usually develop their own commentary based around the script. The following notes follow these lines and give some information about the animals which can be seen from the train. The species are arranged in roughly the order a passenger is likely to see them as the journey proceeds.

Mara
Small animals with grey bodies and tops to their heads, brown chests and sides to their faces and white underparts. Mara, also known as the Patagonian cavy, look somewhat like large rabbits and are sometimes mistaken for small deer. In fact, they are related to guinea-pigs. They are free to roam all over the park, some are usually to be seen in the first paddock between the ha-ha and the road crossing. They live in family groups, pair for life and have communal dens where up to twenty pups from different parents may be left, as in a creche. They come from the pampas grasslands of South America and produce young throughout the year.

Wallaby
The red-necked or Bennett's wallaby are free to roam throughout the park and are often to be seen in the fields to the left of the railway as it leaves the yard and heads towards the first paddock. These animals originate from the brush country of South-East Australia and Tasmania.

Indian Rhinoceros
Once widespread over the Indian sub-continent this species is now confined to national parks. They live on grasslands and flood plains feeding on long lush grass, using their 'prehensile' top lip to put food into their mouths. These animals can be 2 metres tall at the shoulder and weigh 2 tons, but can run at up to 40 mph. The very thick skin protects the animals and folds to allow them to move; the skin within the folds and underneath the body is actually very thin. Their horn is actually compacted hair-like fibre and is never large like the African white rhinoceros. Normally solitary in the wild they only come together for mating. When a female whistles for a male, all within earshot arrive and fight for the right to the female. The horns are not used for fighting - they use large incisor teeth instead.

Gaur
   Although not in the same paddocks as the railway, you may be able to glimpse them in their separate enclosure over on the right shortly after entering the first paddock. They are very large black Asian cattle with horns and mainly come from the forests of India, although some still survive in Burma, Malaysia and Indo-china. The lump on their backs is formed from extensions to their vertebrae and helps them move easily through dense forests.

Pere David's Deer
   A large, light brown deer with antlers which have been described as 'back to front', there being no forward facing point, their survival is an early vindication of captive breeding. Originally they came from China where they are known as mi-lu, which means the 'four unlikes' - supposedly referring to their appearance of having a camel's neck, a stag's antlers, a cow's hoof and a mule's tail! They had been thought to be extinct until in 1865 Pere Armand David, a French missionary, saw some in the Imperial hunting park in Peking (now Beijing) - the only remaining animals. They are therefore named after the man who re-discovered them. Between 1869 and 1890 some live specimens were sent to zoos in the west and in 1895 many of the remainder of the Chinese Royal herd were drowned in floods. During the Boxer rebellion in 1901 most of the remaining animals were killed except for some which were collected and moved out of China. The few surviving animals were gathered into a herd at Woburn by the 11th Duke of Bedford. Subsequently, a second herd was established at Whipsnade (starting with four fawns which arrived at Whipsnade in 1944 for hand rearing) and all the Pere David deer in the world now are descended from these herds. The world population is now over 1,500 animals and a number have been returned to China. Some are in zoos, some live roughly where the old Imperial hunting park was and there is a herd in a reserve in an area where fossil remains show they once lived and where they are now breeding and increasing their numbers. These animals can live for up to 20 years and after a gestation period of nine months it is usual for a single young to be born.

Yak
   These are large, shaggy black cattle from the Tibetan plateaux where they would live at some 13,000 to 20,000 feet altitude. Wild yak are black and now nearly extinct; domestic yak can be black or brown, sometimes with white. The long hair on their sides nearly touches the ground in big males and the bushy tails help to keep them warm. They are able to withstand extremely low temperatures, not even shivering at -18° centigrade; their stomach stays at a constant temperature and acts as a kind of central heating. Domestic yak are used as beasts of burden, being sure-footed in mountainous terrain, they also provide milk. They normally have single young, sometimes twins, after a gestation period of 9 months. Yak are not just used by Tibetans. The Kirghiz, a Turkish Mongolian people, had been forced out of their homelands in Central Asia, going to Afghanistan then Pakistan until the Turkish government airlifted them to an area near Lake Van below Mount Ararat. The yak had traditionally been closely associated with their lives but there are none in Turkey. In 1989

and 1990 Whipsnade sent animals to help these people renew their sense of identity and tradition.

Bactrian Camels

The camels to be seen from the train at Whipsnade are the two-hump bactrian species from northern Asia, but now only found wild in the Gobi Desert area - there may be only 1,000 left in the wild. They have thick coats to protect them from extremes of temperature and a bare belly which radiates body heat into shade. In sand or dust storms their nostrils can be closed and the heavy eyelashes protect their eyes. The large feet help spread their weight on sand and unstable surfaces and although they have hooves they actually walk on the pad behind the hoof rather than on the hoof itself. The humps are fat stores which they can draw on when food is scarce, and have no connection with water, as many people think. The animals can live for 12 to 20 days without water, but can then drink around 30 gallons in a very short time when water is available. They normally have a single calf after a gestation period of 13 months and can live for 30 or more years.

Onager

These animals are one of the Asian wild asses. Although they look like a large, pale brown donkey, they are not the ancestor of the domestic animal. They have an erect black mane and black dorsal stripe and tail tassel. Sometimes called the Persian wild ass, they were once common in Persia (now Iran) and were hunted to a limited extent by the nobility for their meat, and numbers remained stable. Although they are officially protected, this is not effective. Even police and other people in authority have been known to hunt them and the number of animals has declined dramatically. Some onager still live in Russia, which was part of their range, and some have been introduced to reserves in Israel. The males have territories which they defend from other males and form small temporary groups with females during the breeding season.

Blackbuck

These very attractive animals come from the Indian sub-continent, their habitat varying from semi-desert to open woodlands. The males (bucks) develop black underparts when they reach maturity (hence the name) and have long twisting (or spiral) horns. The females and young males are pale fawn with white underparts, females do not have horns. The males mark out territories both conventionally by urine and droppings, but also by marking trees and bushes with a secretion from a gland just below and in front of the eye. The territorial males will tolerate familiar sub-ordinate males provided they remain subordinate. The gestation period is six months and they usually have one young, occasionally two.

Nilgai

These are the largest of the Asian antelopes and come mainly from India where they live in thinly wooded areas. The males are a blue/grey colour (sometimes known as blue bulls) and have short horns, the females are brown and do not have horns. The gestation period is 8 to 9 months and twins are normal. The young are brown, males becoming greyish at about one year-old. Both adults and calves have black and white rings around their feet, white throats and two white spots on the sides of their faces. The cows and calves stay together in herds but males tend to be solitary except in the breeding season.

Axis Deer

These deer are chestnut brown with white spots for camouflage, a dark stripe down the centre of their backs, and white chests. There are no black rump markings. They come from the forests of southern Asia (India and Ceylon) and are also known as spotted deer or chital. They do not have a specific breeding season and males have lyre shaped antlers which are quite large and upright throughout the year. They have a very harsh alarm cry which is used to warn of danger. One of their predators is the Bengal Tiger.

Formosan Sika Deer

There are several races of sika deer throughout Asia. The Formosan race is somewhat different, having evolved on an island isolated from the other types. These animals used to be common in the high central mountains of Formosa, now known as Taiwan. Sadly, their numbers dropped dramatically after the World War II, due to hunting and the destruction of their forest habitat and they came very close to extinction in the wild. Only two herds are known to remain in Taiwan, one on an island and the other in a zoo, and they still are not given proper protection. Fortunately, there are herds in captive collections around the world and one of the largest is at Whipsnade. At first sight they look similar in colouring to axis deer but their coat is a slightly lighter brown and they have a more delicate appearance than axis deer. They have a white rump edged with black and their antlers may appear slightly broadened, but not palmate (flattened) as in fallow deer.

Hog Deer

These dark brown deer come from India, Sri Lanka, Burma, Thailand and Vietnam where they live mainly on open grasslands. They are related to the axis deer, although they do not look very similar, and get their name because their squat appearance with a heavy body and short legs is said to resemble a pig from a distance. They are more solitary than other deer and are usually to be seen singly or in pairs. Only the male has antlers and one or two young are born after a gestation period of seven and a half months.

Fallow Deer

Fallow deer coats vary in colour from nearly white to dark brown, the most common is bright fawn with white spots in summer, fading in winter to grey with faint markings. They have a black line down their back to the tail and black rump markings. These animals were originally natives of Asia Minor and Iran and were introduced into Britain by the Romans. The males (bucks) grow new antlers every year which are used for fighting off rival males and herding up females during the rut (breeding season). The old antlers then drop off and a new set grown the following year. The antlers are distinctive being broad and flattened (known as palmated). The females do not have antlers. The gestation period is about seven and a half months and they usually have a single young, occasionally twins. The young are spotted for camouflage and the mother will hide them under a bush or in long grass and return to feed them. When they grow older and stronger the youngsters will then follow their mother. In the wild, the animals would live for 10 to 12 years, in captivity they can live for up to 25 years.

Chinese Water Deer

A small, plain brown deer about the size of a Labrador dog, they come from China and Korea where they live in swampy and marshland areas. At Whipsnade they are free to wander throughout the park and may be found anywhere. Indeed, the mothers will leave their young in hiding places (different places if there are several young), returning two or three times a day to feed them. Park visitors must not touch a youngster if they come across one since this would result in abandonment by the mother. Multiple births are common, three or four on average but up to eight are possible, the gestation period is about seven months. The males do not have antlers, instead they have long upper canine teeth which are used for fighting, the females do not have these canines.

Muntjac Deer

These deer are very similar to Chinese water deer with a darker brown coat, they also have a dark 'V' on their foreheads. The male has small, simple antlers which are usually shed every year

Barasingha (or Swamp Deer)

These animals are one of the world's largest deer and come from India and Southern Nepal where they live in swampy areas and feed on grasses. Their coat is brown with yellowish underparts, but during the hot season in the wild the stags become a reddish colour. The name means 'twelve tines' and refers to the number of points on their antlers. The gestation period is seven and a half to eight months and the young are spotted, as are most young deer. Recent protection has saved this deer and there are now several collections outside India.

Bar-Headed Geese

These geese come from India and are the white birds with black bars around the head. They can be seen on and around Daedalus Lake.

Black Swan

This easily recognisable swan with black plumage and a red beak is found throughout much of Australia and Tasmania. It has also been introduced to Sweden and New Zealand where it thrives. Swans usually mate for life and both partners raise their brood of cygnets.

Chronology of Key Dates

23rd May, 1931	Whipsnade opened to public
Sept. 1968	End of passenger trains at Bowater's
Oct., 1969	Bowater's ceased to operate their railway
8th May, 1970	Approval in principle to construction of railway
5th August, 1970	Rhinoceros herd arrives at Whipsnade from Africa
26th August, 1970	First train on Whipsnade railway
5th October, 1970	Pleasurerail legally formed
2nd August, 1973	Princess Margaret officially opens full circuit
23rd May, 1981	Duke of Edinburgh rides on railway
28th October, 1990	Last train under Pleasurerail ownership
5th November, 1990	Pleasurerail company officially taken over by zoo

Railway Managers

Summer 1970 to late 1973	Trevor Barber
Late 1973/early 1974 to Nov. 1977	Mrs Elsie Peach
March 1978 to Oct. 1988	Mrs Pauline Haines
1st November, 1988 - Feb. 1994	Frazer Crawley
Feb. 1994 to date	Ian Gordon

Appendix Three

Traffic Figures

Year	Passengers	Zoo Visitors	Percentage of Zoo Visitors	Percentage of Zoo Visitors on Running Days
76/77	103,369	414,779	24.9	26.6
77/78	106,246	400,621	26.5	28.4
78/79	105,073	399,658	26.3	28.8
79/80	98,852	397,366	24.9	27.6
80/81	102,771	392,861	26.2	28.4
81/82	87,306	343,739	25.4	27.8
82/83	91,506	371,762	24.6	26.6
83/84	93,217	384,810	24.2	27.0
84/85	88,633	356,852	24.8	27.1
85/86	91,477	354,594	25.8	28.4
86/87	84,121	379,219	22.2	26.3
87/88	94,754	402,424	23.6	27.0
88/89	92,886	398,953	23.3	27.5
89/90	113,892	455,291	25.0	29.0
90/91*	173,815	485,184	35.8	39.7
91/92*	167,779	430,685	39.0	40.0
93/94	113,272	401,181	28.2	no calc.
94/95	109,151	393,106	27.8	no calc.

* Figures adjusted between seasons due to change in accounting period following acquisition by zoo.

The number of zoo visitors is for attendance over the full year. The percentage of zoo visitors carried is calculated from total attendance. The percentage of visitors carried on running days is an adjusted total taking attendance on days on which the railway actually ran. The variation is not that great since, by definition, the railway is operated when attendance at the zoo is high.

Author's Note

As far as is known, this book is the first attempt to record the history of this fascinating railway. At first, one may assume that with the railway preservation movement well under way when it was first conceived, and a subsequent history of 'just' a quarter of a century, all the facts would be readily available. But it is not as simple as that. The railway has always been operated by minimal permanent staff who were, and are, supplemented by part-time or seasonal staff. The permanent staff have always been hard-pressed to run and maintain a service without much in the way of financial resources. When a locomotive breaks down or has to be taken out of service, busy people know only too well it is in the shed out of action, they do not stop to write it down, the priority being to get it fixed or find another way to serve the queue of people at the ticket office. If a new coach was needed, they got on with building it and getting it out on the line to do useful work. The task of research has been made possible by the complete cooperation and assistance of the current staff who allowed unhindered access to their records. The records all to often, however, are more akin to snippets of information which have to be interpreted, followed by logical assumption after cross-referencing to the recollections of people who worked on the railway, perhaps 20 years ago. As if this were not enough, it is quite clear that not all the records relating to the railway have survived. For instance there is virtually no material relating to staff prior to the 1980s and the information gleaned is, again, a combination of people's memories with a measure of cross reference to known facts such as persons present at meetings or mentioned in letters about other matters. If the result is inaccurate, naturally the responsibility lies with myself as the author.

There will almost certainly be errors or omissions. While every effort has been made to guard against mistakes, it is possible that someone reading this text will have information which corrects the situation as known when the book was written. It is also possible that due credit has not been given to certain people for work they did on the railway. This is probably inevitable when recording a piece of history for the first time. I can say that leads were being followed up and new information included literally within days of the final text being forwarded to the publisher as the deadline approached, the decision having been made to try and publish this record in time for the 25th anniversary of the railway. All the author can ask is that people exercise tolerance in their response and contact me via the publisher in order that the record may be amended or supplemented for the sake of historians who follow.

Acknowledgements

The first and most essential person to whom I must offer my appreciation and thanks is my wife Carolyn. Without her encouragement and support I could not have been in a position to begin this book, without her assistance with field work, note taking and amendments to the text I doubt it would have been completed. The second person to whom grateful thanks must be offered is Ian Gordon, Engineer and General Manager of the railway. Without his patience in constantly answering my questions and the access he freely allowed to the railway and its records the book would have been impossible to prepare. Other staff from Whipsnade Wild Animal Park who provided their help in gathering information include Frances Sutton (development manager) and Graham Lucas (education department). Peter Denton, clerk to the Council & Company Secretary to the Zoological Society of London, also gave enthusiastic assistance to the project, including seeking out archive material and photographs stored at Regents Park. I am grateful to many other people for their time and assistance and thank Sir William McAlpine who, in effect, caused the railway to be built and, with friends, formed Pleasurerail Ltd and remained closely associated with the railway until it was sold to the ZSL, and Tom Hill, also a crucial figure in the construction and early history of the railway. Trevor Barber, the manager of the railway for the first three years offered invaluable help and material, including photographs, of the early years of the life of the railway. Mrs Elsie Peach helped with the story after the line had settled down to the new circuit and Peter Haines offered much information about the middle years of the railway when he and his wife, Pauline, formed the line's management team. Frazer Crawley, who was the railway manager between November 1988 and February 1994 has also been of great assistance, particularly covering the period of, and following, the acquisition of the railway by the ZSL, the development of the 'Steam Up' weekends and clarifying the many projects involving the park and railway which were worked on but never came to fruition. Others who have helped with material, photographs and reminiscences include David Shepherd, OBE, Martin Johnson, Rod McLeod, Graeme Carr, Keith Tyler, Nick Robey, Paul Morris, Mike Wade, Mervyn Turvey and Peter Newman. I am also grateful for the locomotive drawings prepared by Chris Meachen.

When naming individuals who have offered their time and assistance there is always the risk of missing somebody. If this has occurred, please accept my apologies, your contribution was valuable and much appreciated.

Bibliography & References

Bowater's Sittingbourne Railway by Arthur G. Wells
SKLR Stockbook and Guide 1975 - Sittingbourne & Kemsley Light Railway Ltd
The Welshpool & Llanfair Light Railway by Ralph Cartwright and R.T. Russell
Various Journals of the Welshpool & Llanfair Light Railway Society
The Welsh Highland Railway Today, 1975 - Welsh Highland Light Railway (1964) Ltd
Welsh Highland Railway 25th Anniversary Stocklist - Welsh Highland Light Railway (1964) Ltd
Whipsnade Zoo Guide Book, 1981
Whipsnade Wild Animal Park Guide Book, 1994
Whipsnade Wild Animal Park *My Africa* by Lucy Pendar
Great Whipsnade Train Commentary, 1994
A Brush with Steam by David Shepherd, OBE
'Rail' Magazine article by Roger Butcher